COLONIAL SETTLEMENTS
OF
NEW ENGLAND

Towns, Villages and Plantations
(1607 – 1850)
(Partial List)

Researched and Compiled by Steven Herrick

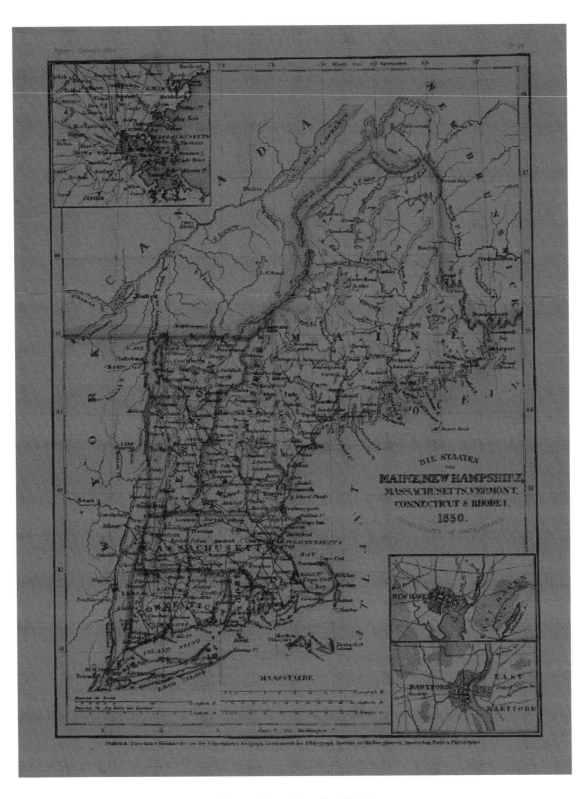

New England 1850

TABLE of CONTENTS

PREFACE

Before I present my compilation, I would be remiss not to mention the Native Americans who settled the subject territory thousands of years prior to the European great migration to New England at the beginning of the 17th Century. The map below shows only the Southern New England native tribal territories c. 1600. A suitable graphic of Northern Tribes was not readily available so the vast lands of the Penobscots, Passamaquoddys, Micmacs and others will be left to the imagination of the reader.

While recognizing there were devastating consequences, this publication does not attempt to address the societal wrongs or rights of such an historic immigration. This work only strives to show the clinical location data of English-speaking settlements underlying which there are many personal tragic events for so many people, native and immigrant.

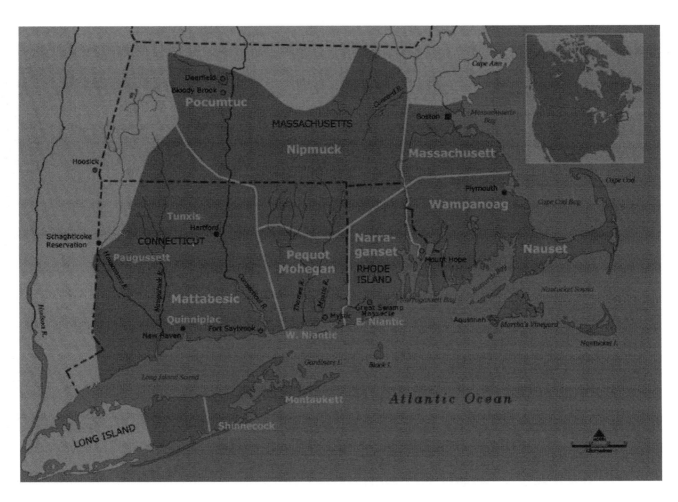

"Tribal Territories Southern New England" by Nikater; adapted to English by Hydrargyrum – Wikimedia Commons - Image:Wohngebiet_Südneuengland.png, as of 5 July 2006. Licensed under CC BY-SA 3.0 via Wikimedia Commons

This project started about 2005 as my family tree began to seriously expand into 17th Century Colonial New England. When I compared dates and towns shown in family published records and other on-line genealogy source material that I obtained, I found a high percentage of incorrect town entries for births, marriages and deaths. I wanted my tree to be as accurate as possible, not only for the integrity of my tree but also as solid reference points for others to use, so I started to record verified historical town, village and plantation data.

My "crib notes" that formed the basis of this publication began with one sticky-note of settlement and incorporation dates for a handful of Essex County, Massachusetts colonial towns. As my tree grew, I soon had many handwritten difficult-to-search sticky-notes on my office wall and realized it was time to start a small database, my first being about three pages. After that, I began to systematically add to my database as I expanded my family tree to what is now over 40,000 people. With that many tree dwellers, my database had reached a penetration plateau with new entries diminishing to a trickle. It was then that I decided to fill in some gaps in my database by researching from the "top down". I began with Maine and Massachusetts town source publications, and integrated many new towns into my database. Following Maine and Massachusetts, I progressed into records of Connecticut, New Hampshire, Rhode Island and Vermont. I had many fewer ancestors in those States so new entries rapidly grew my database as I researched those records.

The original intent of my project was to just compile a list of towns, However, as I did so, I realized that the reader would benefit from a political framework timeline of the New England States. At the beginning of each State chapter, you will see a timeline that I think will be useful. I must say that I learned a great deal about the colonial history of our great country as I progressed with this part of my research.

As the information in this publication significantly helped me increase the accuracy of my tree, I know it will do the same for other amateurs as well as professional genealogists. Please remember the following is a partial list and I would welcome any additions, corrections or comments. Also, I would like to hear positive or negative feedback about the usefulness of this data.

Finally, I want to thank Wikipedia for all the information provided by that website. While I often used that information only to lead me to other verification sources, I have found the Wikipedia entries alone to be very accurate and invaluable to me. I encourage everyone who uses Wikipedia to support that concept by possibly submitting entries, editing entries or by monetary contribution. Millennials may not have heard about Encyclopedia Britannica but I recall the considerable cost of buying a "set" for our children in the 70's plus buying annual volumes of revisions and new entries. Now even better free information is available through Wikipedia on a continuously updated format. May the digital information age continue to flourish!

Steven Herrick, Compiler and Researcher

CHAPTER I
CONNECTICUT

Mohegan name: Quinnetukut

Colonial Era Events in Connecticut

1614: **First European Exploration**; Dutch explorers sailed up the "Connecticut River" at least as far as the Little River (now Parker River), later site of Hartford.

1623: **Dutch Fort on the Little River**; The Dutch West India Company built Foot Hoop on the south bank of the Little River and began trading operations.

1633: **First European Settlement**; The area called Matianuck by the Podunk tribe was offered to settlers from Massachusetts if they would be a mediating force between the Podunk and other larger tribes such as the Pequot and Mohegan. In 1635, this settlement was called Dorchester and, in 1637, it was Inc. as Windsor. The Dutch who proceeded them were either traders or members of the garrison, neither of which could truly be considered "settlers". Matianuck was the beginning of what would be called the Connecticut Colony.

1634: **Wethersfield**; This second European settlement in Connecticut was established just South of where Hartford would later be settled.

1635: **Saybrook Colony**; Separate from the Connecticut Colony, Saybrook Colony was established at the mouth of the Connecticut River.

1636: **More Settlements**; Hartford and Springfield on the upper Connecticut River and Saybrook with its Fort Saybrook were settled.

1637: **First Official Towns**; Windsor and Hartford were Inc.

1638: **New Haven Colony**; Another "Colony" called New Haven Colony is formed along the coast south of the Saybrook Colony

1644: **Two Colonies Merge**; Saybrook Colony merged with Connecticut Colony keeping the name of Connecticut Colony.

1650: **Dutch Pack up and Leave**; Following years of friction, the Dutch concede the area to the British and agree, via the Treaty of Hartford, to withdraw.

1662: Colony Charter Granted; John Winthrop Jr. obtains a <u>self-governing</u> Colony Charter for Connecticut, granted by King Charles II

1665: Colonies Merge; New Haven Colony merged with Connecticut Colony keeping the name of Connecticut Colony.

1686: Dominion of New England; All of the America Colonies from the Delaware River to Penobscot Bay in Maine were declared one entity, Dominion of New England, by King James II. From the outset, there was mass resistance to that concept because the colonists resented being stripped of rights by anyone, let alone a King who had strong ties to the Catholic Church.

1689: Dominion of New England Collapses; After King James II was overthrown in December 1688, the Colonies ousted Dominion officials and reverted to their previous structures and authorities.

1749: Massachusetts Towns Ceded to Connecticut; The Massachusetts towns of Enfield, Somers, Suffield and Woodstock were ceded to **Connecticut** as part of a boundary settlement.

1774: Continental Congress; Connecticut participates in the First Continental Congress.

1778: Connecticut Statehood; Connecticut became the 5th of the 13 original States to ratify the Constitution.

CONNECTICUT SETTLEMENTS

<u>Populated Place:</u>

Agawam P.: Settled in 1636; **See Springfield MA**
Andover: Tolland Co., Prev. to 1848 part of Hebron and Coventry, **Inc. in 1848 as Andover**
Ashford: Windham Co., **Inc. in 1714 as Ashford**
Asquinebaug: Windham Co., **Inc. 1699 as Asquinebaug,** Name changed in 1700 to **Plainfield**
Bedford: Fairfield Co., Settled in 1680 by Stamford Puritans, **Inc. in 1697 as Bedford CT.,**
    Transferred to NY in 1700 per Royal Decree
Berlin: Hartford Co., Settled in 1668, **Inc. in 1785 as Berlin**
Bolton: Tolland Co., **Inc. in 1720 as Bolton**
Branford: New Haven Co., Settlement in 1644 called Totoket a V. in Newhaven, **Inc. in 1685 as Branford**
Bristol: Hartford Co., **Inc. in 1785 as Bristol**
Canaan: Litchfield Co., **Inc. in 1759 as Canaan**
Canterbury: Windham Co., Settled in 1680 as part of Plainfield, **Inc. in 1703 as Canterbury**
Chester: Middlesex Co., Settlement in 1692 called Pattaconk Quarter, **Inc. in 1836 as Chester**
Colchester: New London Co., Settlement in 1692 called Jeremiah's Farm, **Inc. 1699 as Colchester**
Columbia: Tolland Co., Prev. to 1804 part of Lebanon, **Inc. in 1804 as Columbia**
Coventry; Tolland Co., Settled in 1709, **Inc. in1712 as Coventry**

Derby: New Haven Co., Settlement in 1642 called Paugasset, Called Derby in 1675, **Inc. 1775 as Derby**

Dorchester: Hartford Co. Settled in 1633, **See Windsor**

Durham: Middlesex Co., Settled in1699, **Inc. in 1708 as Durham**

East Haddam: Middlesex Co., Prev. to 1734 part of Haddam, Settled in 1734 as East Haddam, **Inc. in 1734 as East Haddam**

East Saybrook P.: New London Co., Settled in 1665, **See Lyme and Old Lyme**

East Windsor: Hartford Co., Settled in 1670, **See South Windsor**

Elizabeth's Neck: Fairfield Co., Settled in 1640, **See Greenwich**

Enfield: Hartford Co., Settled in 1679 as a V. in Hampshire Co., **MA., Inc. in 1683 as Enfield MA, Ceded in 1749 to CT.**

Fairfield: Fairfield Co., Prev. to 1639 called Pequannocke, Settled in 1639, **Inc. in 1685 as Fairfield**

Farmington: Hartford Co., Settled in 1641, **Inc. in 1645 as Farmington**

Glastonbury: Hartford Co., Settlement in 1636 called Pyquag on the east bank of the Connecticut River, **Inc. in 1693 as Glastonbury**

Greenwich: Fairfield Co., Settlement in 1640 called Elizabeth's Neck, **Inc. in 1665 as Greenwich**, In 1677 the court awarded 5,000 acres of Greenwich to **RI** that was Inc. in 1677 as East Greenwich **RI**

Griswold: New London Co., Settled in 1669 as part of Preston, Called North Society in 1715, **Inc. in 1815 as Griswold**

Groton: New London Co., Settled in 1646 as part of New London, **Inc. in 1705 as Groton**

Guilford: New Haven Co., Settled in 1639, **Inc. in 1643 as Guilford**

Haddam: Middlesex Co., Settlement in 1662 called Plantation at Thirty Mile Island, **Inc. in 1668 as Haddam**

Hammonasset: Middlesex Co., Settled in 1663, **See Killingworth**

Hampton: Windham Co., **Inc. in 1786 as Hampton**

Hartford: Hartford Co., Settlement in 1636 called Newtown, **Inc. in 1637 as Hartford**

Hastings: Fairfield Co., Settled in 1660, **See Rye**

Hebron: Tolland Co., Settled in Hartford Co. in 1699, **Inc. in 1708 as Hebron** in Hartford Co., In Windham Co. in 1726, In Tolland Co. in 1785

Jeremiah's Farm: New London Co., Settled in 1692, **See Colchester**

Kenilworth: Middlesex Co., Settlement in 1663 called Hammonasset, **Inc. in 1667 as Kenilworth,** Called Killingworth about 1750, **Name officially changed in 1838 to Killingworth**

Kent: Litchfield Co., **Inc. in 1739 as Kent**

Killingly: Windham Co., **Inc. in 1708 as Killingly**

Killingworth: Middlesex Co., Settlement in 1663 called Hammonasset, **Inc. in 1667 as Kenilworth,** Called Killingworth about 1750, **Name officially changed in 1838 to Killingworth**

Lebanon: New London Co., Settlement in 1663 called Pomakuck, **Inc. in 1700 as Lebanon,** Note: (From 1726 to 1824 Lebanon was in Windham Co.)

Litchfield: Litchfield Co., **Inc. in 1719 as Litchfield**

Lyme: New London Co., Settlement in 1665 called East Saybrook P., **Inc. in 1667 as Lyme**, See Old Lyme

Mansfield: Tolland Co., Settled in 1692 as part of Windham, **Inc. in 1702 as Mansfield**

Manursing Island: Fairfield Co., Settlement in 1660 called Hastings on Manursing I., **See Rye**

Marlboro: Hartford Co. **Alias of Marlborough**

Marlborough: Hartford Co.; Settled in 1648 as part of Glastonbury, Colchester and Hebron; **Inc. in 1803 as Marlborough** aka Marlboro

Matianuck: Hartford Co., Settled in **1633** as the 1st European Settlement in CT, **See Windsor**

Mattatuck: New Haven Co., Settled in 1674, **See Waterbury**

Middletown: Middlesex Co., Settled in 1650, **Inc. in 1651as Middletown**

Milford: New Haven Co., Settlement in 1639 called Wepawaug, **Inc. in 1640 as Milford**

Montville: New London Co., Settled in 1646 as part of the V. of Pequot, Called Montville V. in 1658 in New London, **Inc. in 1786 as Montville**

Mystic Village: New London Co., Settled about 1640 after the Pequot War and is still a V. within the towns of Groton and Stonington

Mystick: New London Co., Settlement in 1649 called Stonington **MA**, Called Souther Towne **MA** (aka Southerton) in 1658, **Inc. in 1662 as Stonington CT, Name changed in 1665 to Mystick, Name changed in 1666 back to Stonington, See Stonington**

New Britain: Hartford Co., Settled in 1687, **Inc. in 1850 as New Britain**

New Hartford: Litchfield Co., Settled in 1733, **Inc. in 1738 as New Hartford**

New Haven: New Haven Co., Settlement in 1638 called Quinnipiac, Called Newhaven in 1640, **Inc. in 1664 as New Haven**

New London: New London Co., Settlement in 1646 called Pequot, **Inc. in 1658 as New London**

New Milford: Litchfield Co., Settled in 1707, **Inc. in1712 as New Milford**

Newhaven: New Haven Co., Settled in 1638, **See New Haven**

Newtown (1): Hartford Co., Settled in1635, **See Hartford**

Newtown (2): Fairfield Co., **Inc. in 1711 as Newtown**

North Society: New London Co., Settled in 1669, **See Griswold**

Northbury: Litchfield Co., Settled in 1740 as a V. in Waterbury, **See Plymouth**

Norwalk: Fairfield Co., Settled in 1640, **Inc. in 1651 as Norwalk**

Norwich: New London Co., Settled in 1658, **Inc. in 1662 as Norwich, Inc. in 1784 as the City of Norwich**

Old Lyme: New London Co., Settlement in 1665 called East Saybrook P., Part of Lyme in 1667, **Inc. in 1855 as South Lyme, 1857 renamed Old Lyme in 1857**

Old Saybrook: Middlesex Co., Settlement in 1635 called Saybrook P., **Inc. in 1854 as Old Saybrook**

Oneco: Windham Co., A V. in Sterling

Pattaconk Quarter: Middlesex Co., Settled in 1692, **See Chester**

Paugasset: New Haven Co., Settled in 1642, **See Derby**

Pequannocke: Fairfield Co., Settled in 1639, **See Fairfield**

Pequot: New London Co., Settled in 1646, **See New London and Montville**

Plainfield: Windham Co., Settled in 1699, **Inc. in 1699 as Asquinebaug, Name changed in 1700 to Plainfield**

Plantation at Thirty Mile Island: Middlesex Co., Settled in 1662, **See Haddam**

Plymouth: Litchfield Co., Settlement in 1740 called Northbury V. in Waterbury, **Inc. in 1795 as Plymouth**

Pomakuck: New London Co., Settled in 1663, **See Lebanon**

Pomfret: Windham Co., **Inc. in 1713 as Pomfret**

Preston: New London Co., Settled in 1686, **Inc. in 1687 as Preston**

Pyquag: Hartford Co., Settled in1636, **See Glastonbury**

Quinebaug: Windham Co., **Inc. in 1699 as Quinebaug, See Plainfield**

Quinnipiac: New Haven Co., Settled in1638, **See New Haven**

Ridgefield: Fairfield Co., Settled in 1708, **Inc in 1709 as Ridgefield**

Rippowam: Fairfield Co., Settled in 1641, **See Stamford**

Rye: Fairfield Co., Prev. to 1660 called Manursing I, Settlement in 1660 called Hastings, **Inc. in 1663 as Rye CT, Ceded in 1683 to NY, Rejoined CT in 1695, Ceded to NY in 1700 by Royal decree**

Salisbury: Litchfield Co., Settled in 1728, **Inc. in 1741 as Salisbury**

Saybrook P.: Middlesex Co., Settled in 1635, **See Old Saybrook**

Simsbury: Hartford Co., Settled in 1670, **Inc. in 1670 as Simsbury**

Somers: Tolland Co., Settlement in 1734 called East Enfield a V. in Springfield **MA**, **Inc. 1734 as Somers MA, Ceded in 1749 to CT**

South Lyme: New London Co., Settled in1665 as a V. in Lyme, **Inc. in 1855 as South Lyme, Renamed Old Lyme in 1857**

South Windsor: Hartford Co., Part of Windsor in 1670, Called East Windsor in 1768, **Inc. in 1854 as South Windsor**

Souther Towne: New London Co., Settlement in 1649 as Souther Towne aka Southerton, **See Stonington**

Southerton: New London Co., **Alias of Souther Towne**

Stafford: Tolland Co., **Inc. in 1719 as Stafford**

Stamford: Fairfield Co., Settlement in 1641 called Rippowam, **Inc. in 1662 as Stamford**

Sterling: Windham Co., **Inc. in 1794 as Sterling**

Stonington: New London Co., Called Stonington **MA** in 1649, Called Souther Towne (aka Southerton) **MA** in 1658, **Inc. in 1662 as Stonington CT, Renamed Mystick in 1665, Renamed Stonington in 1666**

Stratford: Fairfield Co., Settled in 1639, **Inc. in 1639 as Stratford**

Suffield: Hartford Co., Settlement in 1674 called Southfield **MA**, **Inc. in 1682 as Suffield in Hampden Co. MA, Ceded to CT in 1749**

Terryville: Litchfield Co., Settled in1740 as a V. in Plymouth

Thompson: Windham Co., Settled in 1729, **Inc. in 1785 as Thompson**

Tolland: Tolland Co., Settled in 1715, **Inc. in 1722 as Tolland**

Torrington: Litchfield Co., Settlement in 1735 called Wolcottville, **Inc. in 1740 as Torrington**

Totoket: New Haven Co., Settled in 1644, **See Branford**

Voluntown: New London Co., Settlement in 1708 called Volunteer Town, **Inc. in 1721 as Voluntown,** In Windham Co. in 1721, In New London Co. in 1881

Wallingford: New Haven Co., Prev. to 1667 part of New Haven, Called Wallingford V. in 1667, **Inc. in 1670 as Wallingford**

Waterbury: New Haven Co., Settlement in 1674 called Mattatuck, Deserted in 1675 due to French and Indian War, Resettled in 1677, **Inc. in 1686 as Waterbury**

Watertown: Litchfield Co., Settled in1684, **Inc. in 1780 as Watertown**

Weathersfield: Hartford Co., **Alias of Wethersfield**

Wepawaug: New Haven Co., Settled in 1639, **See Milford**

Wethersfield: Hartford Co., Settlement in 1634, **Inc. in 1822 as Wethersfield** aka Weathersfield

Willington: Tolland Co., **Inc. in 1727 as Willington**

Windham: Windham Co., **Inc. in 1692 as Windham**

Windsor: Hartford Co., Settlement in 1633 called Matianuck, Called Dorchester in 1635, **Inc. in 1637 as Windsor**

Wolcottville: Litchfield Co., Settled in 1735, **See Torrington**

Woodbury: Litchfield Co., Settled in 1673, **Inc. in 1674 as Woodbury**

Woodstock: Windham Co., Settlement in 1686 called New Roxbury in Worcester Co. **MA**, Called Woodstock **MA** in 1690, **Ceded to CT and Inc. in 1749 as Woodstock CT**

CHAPTER II
MAINE

Within five years of the first European settlements in what would become Maine
"The Great Dying" epidemic spread from Penobscot Bay westward
claiming the lives of an estimated 75% of the native population.

Colonial Era Events in Maine

1606: **First Virginia Charter**; Present-day Southern Maine, from the Piscataqua to Kennebec Rivers was included as part of the 1606 First Virginia Charter granted to the Virginia Company of Plymouth.

1607: **English Colonists;** An attempt was made to establish Popham Colony, aka Sagadahoc Colony, at present-day Phippsburg, Maine. After a harsh winter, all the surviving settlers returned to England in 1608 on the pinnace *Virginia,* the first ship built in "Maine".

1611: **French Mission;** Father Pierre Biard started a Catholic Jesuit Mission on Indian Island in the Penobscot River near Old Town, Maine.

1613: **French Mission;** A second Jesuit Mission was started on Mount Desert Island at Fernald's Point in present-day Southwest Harbor, Maine.

1613: **French Trading Post;** French traders from Port Royal, Nova Scotia, establish a trading post called Bagaduce at Majorbigwaduce in present-day Castine.

1616: **"The Great Dying" Epidemic;** A widespread epidemic spread from Penobscot Bay Westward among Native Americans. It is estimated that at least 75% of their population died between 1616 and 1619. This dreadful process was not limited to 17th Century New England but occurred throughout the Americas following the arrival of Europeans. For example, ALL native Caribbean people had disappeared within 50 years of the arrival of Columbus.

1621: **First English Traders;** The Kennebunk trading post was established by the Plymouth Council for New England and later developed into Kennebunk Village within Wells Plantation in 1643.

1622: **Province of Maine;** The Plymouth Council for New England established the Province of Maine, which included all land from the Merrimack to Kennebec Rivers.

1623: **Isles of Shoals (9 habitable islands);** Five of the nine islands settled by fishermen and their families starting in 1623 would eventually become part of Maine. The other four islands would become part of New Hampshire.

1628: **Cushnoc Trading Post;** The first charter of a Massachusetts Fur Trading Post was granted for <u>settlers</u> at Cushnoc (now Augusta). It was abandoned by 1661.

1629: **Grant to John Mason;** John Mason was granted the Province of Maine territory from Merrimack to Piscataqua Rivers and he promptly named it New Hampshire.

1629: **New Somersetshire;** What remains of the Province of Maine (Piscataqua to Kennebec Rivers) stays under the control of Massachusetts Bay Colony (MBC) and is called New Somersetshire.

1635: **Fort Pentagoët;** The French constructed Fort Pentagoët at what is now Castine.

1636: **York County;** New Somersetshire (from Piscataqua to Kennebec Rivers) was renamed York County by MBC.

1639: **Gorges Patent;** A Royal Patent of "York County" from King Charles I was granted to Sir Ferdinando Gorges who promptly renames it Province of Maine.

1652: **MBC Claims Province of Maine;** Gorges Patent territory claimed by MBC again calling it York County.

1660: **Court Decision;** The dispute of the ownership of York County is decided in court and it rules in favor of the heirs of Sir Ferdinando Gorges.

1673: **Gorges' heirs sell;** The heirs of Sir Ferdinando sell York County to MBC.

1686: **Dominion of New England;** All of the America Colonies from the Delaware River to Penobscot Bay in Maine were declared one entity, Dominion of New England, by King James II. From the outset, there was mass resistance to that concept because the colonists resented being stripped of rights by anyone, let alone a King who had strong ties to the Catholic Church.

1689: **Dominion of New England Collapses;** After King James II was overthrown in December 1688, the Colonies ousted Dominion officials and reverted to their previous structures and authorities.

1760: **Cumberland County:** Cumberland County is established from the present-day eastern border of York County to east of Casco Bay.

1760: **Lincoln County;** About 60% of today's Maine (Casco Bay to Canada) is designated as Lincoln County. So, in 1760, the Province of Maine made up of three counties, York, Cumber and Lincoln.

1780: **District of Maine;** MBC changed the title of "Maine" from the Province of Maine to District of Maine. I expect this was done to show that "Maine" was under the control of MBC.

1789: **Hancock County Established;** Split from the Lincoln County

1789: **Washington County Established;** Split from Lincoln Co.

1799: **Kennebec County Established;** Created from parts of Cumberland and Lincoln Counties

1805: **Oxford County Established;** First land-locked County

1820: **State of Maine Established;** Maine statehood was created by Congress as the 23rd State of the Union by the Missouri Compromise whereby Massachusetts ceded its authority over the "District of Maine", which by 1820, including the counties of Cumberland, Devonshire (defunct), Hancock, Kennebec, Lincoln, Oxford, Penobscot, Somerset, Washington and York.

1827: **Waldo County Established;** Split from Hancock Co.

1838: **Piscataquis County Established;** Split from West Penobscot and East Somerset Counties

1839: **Aroostook County Established;** Formed from parts of Penobscot and Washington Counties

1854: **Sagadahoc County Established;** Split from Lincoln County

1854: **Androscoggin County Established;** Formed from parts of Cumberland, Lincoln, Kennebec and Oxford Counties

1860: **Knox County Established;** Formed from parts of Waldo and Lincoln Counties

----

MAINE SETTLEMENTS

All events prior to 1820 occurred in Plymouth Colony (1620-1629), Massachusetts Bay Colony (1630-1690), Province of Massachusetts Bay (1691-1787) and State of Massachusetts (1788-1819).

Populated Place:

Abbot: Piscataquis Co., **Inc. in 1827 as Abbot**
Acton: York Co., Settlement in 1776 called Acton V., Called Acton V. in Shapleigh in 1785, **Inc in 1830 as Acton**
Addison: Washington Co., Prev. to 1797 called Plantation # 6, **Inc. in 1797 as Addison**
Agamenticus: York Co., Settlement in 1624 called Agamenticus P., Called Bristol (not the Bristol in Lincoln Co.) in 1636, **Inc. in 1642 as "City of Gorgeana"**, the first "city" in New England by King Charles I's Royal Decree, **See York**
Albion: Kennebec Co., Settlement in 1802 called Freetown P. (2), **Inc. in 1804 as Fairfax, Renamed Ligonia in 1821, Renamed Albion in 1824**
Alna: Lincoln Co., Settled in 1760 as part of Pownalborough, **Inc. in 1794 as New Milford, Renamed Alna in 1811**
Amherst: Hancock Co., Prev. to 1831 part of Plantation # 26, **Inc. in 1831 as Amherst**
Andover: Oxford Co., Settlement called East Andover P. in 1789, **Inc. in 1804 as <u>East</u> Andover, Renamed in 1820 as Andover**
Appledore: York Co., First settled in 1623, Part of Kittery in 1647, All nine of the habitable islands in

the Isles of Shoals were **Inc. in 1661 as Appledore by Massachusetts Bay Colony,** Five would eventually end up in **ME** (Appledore, Smuttynose, Malaga, Cedar and Duck), The other four would end up in **NH.**

Appledore Island: York Co., Settled in 1623, 1 of 5 ME islands in the Isles of Shoals, **See Appledore & Isles of Shoals**

Appleton: Knox Co., Settlement in 1821 called Appleton P., **Inc. in 1829 as Appleton**

Appleton P.: Knox Co., **See Appleton**

Arrowseag Island: Sagadahoc Co., **See Arrowsic**

Arrowsic: Sagadahoc Co., Prev. to 1657 called Arrowseag Island, Settlement in 1657 called Arrowsic, Indian massacre in 1676 destroyed fort and town, Resettled in 1679 and called Newtown, Newtown destroyed in 1689 by Indians and abandoned by settlers, Resettled in 1714 and called Newtown-on-Arrowsic, In 1716 part of the town of Georgetown-on-Arrowsic aka Georgetown, Split from Georgetown-on-Arrowsic and **Inc. in 1841 as Arrowsic**

Arundel: York Co., Settled and **Inc. in 1653 as Cape Porpus,** Deserted about 1689, Resettled about 1700, **Inc. in 1719 as Arundel,** Name changed in **1821 to Kennebunk** aka Kennebunkport

Augusta: Kennebec Co., Settlement in 1754 called Cushnoc, Part of Hallowell in 1771, Split from Hallowell in and **Inc. in Feb 1797 as Harrington, Name changed Jun 1797 to Augusta**
Note: (In Jun 1797 a portion of P. # 5 in Washington Co. was split off and Inc. as Harrington.)

Aurora: Hancock Co., Prev. to 1831 part of P. # 27, **Inc. in 1831 as Hampton** aka Richards, **Renamed Aurora in 1833**

Bagaduce: See Castine

Bakersfield P.: Androscoggin Co., **See Poland**

Baldwin: Cumberland Co., Settlement in 1774 called Flintstown, **Inc. in 1802 as Baldwin**

Bangor: Penobscot Co., Settlement in 1769 called Condeskeag, **Inc. in 1791 as Bangor, Inc. in 1834 as City of Bangor**

Bar Harbor: Hancock Co., Settled in 1763 as part of Mount Desert P., **Inc. in 1796 as Eden, Renamed Bar Harbor in 1918**

Bar Mills: York Co., A V. in Buxton

Barretstown P.: Knox Co., **See Hope**

Bass Harbor: Hancock Co., Settled in 1762 as part of Tremont, Called McKinley V. in Tremont in 1900, Called Bass Harbor V. in Tremont in 1961

Bath: Sagadahoc Co., Settled in 1649 as part of Georgetown, **Inc. in 1781 as Bath, Inc. in 1847 as the City of Bath**

Beaver Hill P.: Waldo Co., **See Freedom**

Beddington: Washington Co., **Inc. in 1833 as Beddington,** Note: (Smallest population of any town Inc. in Maine with 50 residents in 2010)

Belfast: Waldo Co., Part of Muscongus Patent in 1630, Part of the Waldo Patent in 1720, Prev. to 1770 known as Passagassawakeag, Settlement called Belfast in 1770 by new Scotch-Irish owners, **Inc. in 1773 as Belfast,** Destroyed by British Military in 1779 who later "held" the town for 5 days in 1814, **Inc. in 1853 as City of Belfast**

Belgrade: Kennebec Co., Settlement in 1774 called Washington P., **Inc. in 1796 as Belgrade**

Belmont: Waldo Co., Prev. to 1814 part of Green P., **Inc. in 1814 as Belmont**

Bernard: Hancock Co., **See Tremont**

Berwick: York Co., Part of Piscataqua P. in 1631, Settlement called Berwick V. in Kittery in 1635 aka North Parish & Kittery Commons, **Inc. in 1713 as Berwick**

Bethel: Oxford Co., Unsettled V. in 1769 within Sudbury Canada P., Settlement called Bethel in 1774, **Inc. in 1796 as Bethel**

Biddeford: York Co., Settled in 1631 as part of Winter Harbor, Part of Saco in 1653, Called Biddeford in 1718, **Inc. in 1728 as Biddeford**

Birch Harbor: Hancock Co., **V. in Gouldsboro**

Black Point: Cumberland Co., Settlement in 1631 called Black Point, **See Black Point Patent and Scarborough**

Black Point Patent: Cumberland Co., A 1630 Land Grant that would eventually have 4 villages; Black Point, Blue Point, Dunstan & Stratton; All Inc. in 1658 as Scarborough

Blaisdelltown: Penobscot Co., **See Exeter**

Blakesburg P.: Penobscot Co., Settled in 1824, **See Bradford**

Bloomfield: Somerset Co., **Inc. in 1814 as Bloomfield, Annexed by Skowhegan in 1861**

Blue Hill: Hancock Co., Settled in 1762 as Blue Hill Bay P. in Lincoln Co. aka Newport P., **Inc. in 1789 as Blue Hill** in Hancock Co.

Blue Hill Bay P.: Hancock Co., **See Blue Hill**

Blue Point: Cumberland Co., Settlement in 1631 called Blue Point. **See Black Point Patent and Scarborough**

Boothbay: Lincoln Co., Settlement in 1730 called Townsend, **Inc. in 1764 as Townsend, Renamed Boothbay in 1842**

Boothbay Harbor: Lincoln Co., Settled in 1730 as part of Townsend V., Part of Town of Townsend in 1764, Part of Boothbay in 1842, **Inc. in 1889 as Boothbay Harbor**

Bowdoin: Sagadahoc Co., Part of West Bowdoinham P. in 1770, **Inc. in 1788 as Bowdoin**

Bowdoinham: Sagadahoc Co., Settled in 1720, Deserted in 1723 due to Dummer's War, Resettled in 1730, **Inc. in 1762 as Bowdoinham**

Bradford: Penobscot Co., Settlement in 1824 called Blakesburg P., **Inc. in 1831 as Bradford**

Bradley: Penobscot Co., Settlement in 1796 called Township # 4 EPR, **Inc. in 1834 as Bradley**

Brewer: Penobscot Co., Prev. to 1812 part of Orrington, **Inc. in 1812 as Brewer**

Bridges P.: Waldo Co., **See Troy**

Bristol (1): York Co., Settled in 1624, **See York**

Bristol (2): Lincoln Co., Settlement in 1625 called Pemaquid a year-round Trading Post, Called Pemaquid Patent of Plymouth Colony in 1631, Called Pemaquid in York Co. in 1636., Called Jamestown in York Co. in 1664, Called Pemaquid in newly formed Lincoln Co. in 1760, **Inc. in 1765 as Bristol**

Bristol Mills: Lincoln Co., V. in Bristol (2) in 1765

Broad Bay: Lincoln Co., Settled in 1733, **See Waldoborough**

Brooklin: Hancock Co., Settlement in 1759 called Naskeag, Part of Sedgwick in 1789, **Inc. on 09 Jun 1849 as Port Watson, Renamed Brooklin on 23 July 1849**

Brooksville: Hancock Co.; Settled in 1764 as part of Castine, Penobscot and Sedgwick; **Inc. in 1817 as Brooksville**

Brownfield: Oxford Co., Settlement in 1765 called Brownfield P., **Inc. in 1802 as Brownfield**

Brownfield P.: Oxford Co., **See Brownfield**

Brunswick: Cumberland Co., Settlement in 1628 called Pejepscot, Called Brunswick P. in 1717, **Inc. in 1739 as Brunswick**

Brunswick P.: Cumberland Co., **See Brunswick**

Buckfield: Oxford Co., Settlement in 1776 called Buckfield P., **Inc. in 1793 as Buckfield**

Buckfield P.: Oxford Co., **See Buckfield**

Bucks Harbor: Washington Co., A V. in Machiasport in 1763

Bucksport: Hancock Co., Settlement in 1763 called Plantation # 1, Called Buckstown P. in 1783, **Inc. in 1792 as Buckstown, Renamed Bucksport in 1817**

Buckstown: Hancock Co., Settlement in 1763 called Plantation # 1, Called Buckstown P. in 1783, **Inc. 1792 as Buckstown, See Bucksport**

Buckstown P.: Hancock Co., **See Bucksport & Buckstown**

Buxton: York Co., Unsettled in 1728 but called Narragansett # 1, Settlement in 1750 called Buxton, **Inc.**

in 1772 as Buxton

Buxton Center: York Co., A.V. in Buxton

Camden: Knox Co., Settlement in 1770 called Mcgunicook P., **Inc. in 1791 as Camden**

Canaan: Somerset Co., Settlement in 1770 called Wesserunsett aka Heywoodstown, **Inc. in 1788 as Canaan**

Canaan P.: Waldo Co., **See Lincolnville**

Cape Elizabeth: Cumberland Co., Trading post in 1628, Settlement in 1630 called Purpooduc in area called New Casco, Part of the area called Falmouth in 1658, **Inc. in 1765 as Cape Elizabeth District., Renamed in 1775 as Cape Elizabeth**

Cape Neddick: York Co., Settled in 1654, A.V. in York

Cape Newagan Island: Lincoln Co., Settled in 1623 as a fishing and trading V., **See Southport**

Cape Porpoise: York Co., **Alias of Cape Porpus**

Cape Porpus: York Co., Named in 1614 by Capt. John Smith, Settled in 1623, **Inc. in 1653 as Cape Porpus**

Casco: Cumberland Co., **See Falmouth and Portland**

Castine: Hancock Co., Called Majorbigwaduce in 1613 by French Missionaries, Called Pentagoët in 1625, Seized from the French by English Colonists from Plymouth Colony in 1628, Called Bagaduce in 1667, Called Penobscot in 1704, Called Twp. # 3 EPR in 1762 aka Majorbigwaduce P., Called New Ireland in 1779, Called Castine V. in Penobscot in1787, **Inc. in 1796 as Castine**

Cedar Island: York Co., 1 of 5 Maine islands in the Isles of Shoals in 1623, **See Appledore & Isles of Shoals**

Centreville: Washington Co., Settlement in 1770 called Township # 23, aka Centerville, **Inc. in 1842 as Centreville**, Its town charter was terminated in 2004 and Centrevillle became an Unorganized Territory in North Washington Co.

Chamberlain: Lincoln Co., A.V. in Bristol settled in 1765

Charlotte: Washington Co., Prev. to 1825 called P. # 3, **Inc. in 1825 as Charlotte**

Cherryfield: Washington Co., Settled in 1757 as part of P. # 5, Part of Steuben in 1795, **Inc. in 1816 as Cherryfield**

Chicopee: York Co., A.V. in Buxton

China: Kennebec Co., Settlement in 1774 called Jones P., **Inc. in 1796 as Harlem**, Harlem and parts of Fairfax & Winslow **Inc. in 1818 as China**

Clifton: Penobscot Co., Settlement in 1815 called Clifton, **Inc. in 1848 as "Maine", Name changed to Clifton in 1849**

Cold Stream: Penobscot Co., **See Enfield**

Columbia: Washington Co., Settlement in 1770 as Columbia V. in Township # 12, **Inc. in 1796 as Columbia**

Columbia Falls: Washington Co., Settlement in 1770 as Columbia Falls V. in Township # 13, A.V. in Columbia in 1796, **Inc. in 1863 as Columbia Falls**

Corea: Hancock Co., A.V. in Gouldsboro

Cornish: York Co., Trading Post in 1665 called Francisborough, Called Francistown in 1782, **Inc. in 1794 as Cornish**

Coxhall: York Co., Settlement in 1767 called Swanfield, **Inc. in 1780 as Coxhall, Name changed in 1803 to Lyman**

Cranberry Isles: Hancock Co., Settled in1764 in Lincoln Co., Part of town of Mount Desert in 1789 in Hancock Co., **Inc. in 1830 as Cranberry Isles**

Criehaven Island: Knox Co., Settlement in 1754 called Ragged Arse Island, Org. in 1987 as Criehaven Island P., Dissolved in 1925 to an Unorganized Territory

Criehaven Island P.: Knox Co., Settled in 1754, **See Criehaven Island**

Crosbytown: Penobscot Co., Settled in 1807, **See Etna**

Cumberland: Cumberland Co., Settled in 1623 as part of Piscataqua P., Called Cumberland V. in 1652 in Kittery, Called Cumberland V. in1680 in North Yarmouth, **Inc. in 1822 as Cumberland**

Cushing: Knox Co., Settled in 1736 as part of St. Georges P., **Inc. in 1789 as Cushing**

Cushnoc: Kennebec Co., Settled in 1754, **See Augusta**

Cutler: Washington Co., Settled in1826 as a V. in Plantation # 11, **Inc. in 1843 as Cutler**

Damariscotta: Lincoln Co., Settled in 1640 as a V. in Bristol by colonists from Pemaquid V. in Bristol, Damariscotta along with parts of Bristol and Nobleboro were combined and **Inc. in 1848 as Damariscotta**

Dark Harbor: Waldo Co., Settled in 1769 as a V. in Islesborough

Davistown P.: Waldo Co., Settled in 1780, **See Montville & Liberty**

Dedham: Hancock Co., **Inc. in 1837 as Dedham**

Deer Isle: Hancock Co., Settled in 1762 as part of Deer Isle P., **Inc. in 1789 as Deer Isle**

Deer Isle P.: Hancock Co., Settled in 1762, **See Deer Isle & Isle au Haut**

Denmark: Oxford Co., **Inc. in 1807 as Denmark**

Dennysville: Washington Co., Settled in 1786, **Inc. in 1818 as Dennysville**

Dresden: Lincoln Co., Settled in 1752 as part of Frankfort P., Part of Pownalborough in 1760, **Inc. in 1794 as Dresden**

Duck Island: York Co., 1 of 5 Maine islands in the Isles of Shoals in 1623, **See Appledore & Isles of Shoals,** Note: (Duck Island has never been settled)

Ducktrap and Canaan P.: Waldo Co., **See Lincolnville & Northport**

Dunstan: Cumberland Co., Settled in 1631 as a V. in Black Point Patent, **See Scarborough**

East Livermore: Androscoggin Co., Settled in1786 as part of Livermore, **Inc. in 1844 as East Livermore** in Kennebec Co., In Androscoggin Co. in 1854, **Renamed Livermore Falls in 1930**

East Machias: Washington Co., Settled in 1768 as part of Machias, **Inc. in 1826 as East Machias, Name changed in 1840 to Mechisses, Name changed in 1841 back to East Machias**

East Pond P.: Penobscot Co., Settled in1808, **See Newport**

East Thomaston: Knox Co., Settlement called Lemond's Cove in 1769 within St. George's P., Called Shore V. in Thomaston in 1777, **Inc. in 1848 as East Thomaston, Name changed to Rockland in 1850**

Eastport: Washington Co., Settled in 1772 as part of Plantation # 8, **Inc. in 1798 as Eastport,** Note: (Claimed and occupied by the British from 1814 to 1818)

Eddington: Penobscot Co., Settlement in 1778 by Col. Jonathan Eddy and other Nova Scotia Canada residents who supported the USA during the Revolutionary War., **Inc. in 1811 as Eddington**

Eden: Hancock Co., Settled in 1763 as part of the town of Mount Desert, **Inc. in 1796 as Eden, Renamed Bar Harbor in 1918**

Eden Village: Hancock Co., Settled in 1763 as part of the town of Mount Desert, Inc. as Eden in 1796, A V. in Bar Harbor in 1918

Edgecomb: Lincoln Co., Settled in 1744 as part of Freetown P., **Inc. in 1774 as Edgecomb**

Edmunds: Washington Co., Settled in 1775 as part of P. # 10 and Trescott, **Inc. in 1828 as Edmunds,** Edmunds' town charter was terminated in 1937 and it became an Unorganized Territory

Eliot: York Co., Settlement in 1623 called Garden of Kittery, **Inc. in 1810 as Eliot**

Ellsworth: Hancock Co., Settlement in 1763 called Union River Settlement, Organized as P. Number Seven about 1780, **Inc. in 1800 as town of Ellsworth, Inc. in 1869 as City of Ellsworth**

Enfield: Penobscot Co., Settlement in 1820 called Cold Stream, **Inc. in 1835 as Enfield**

Etna: Penobscot Co., Settlement in 1807 called Crosbytown, **Inc. in 1820 as Etna**

Exeter: Penobscot Co., Settlement prev. to 1811 called Blaisdelltown, **Inc. in 1811 as Exeter**

Fairfax: Kennebec Co., Settlement in 1802 called Freetown P., **Inc. in 1804 as Fairfax, Renamed**

Ligonia in 1821, Renamed Albion in 1824

Falmouth: Cumberland Co., Part of the area called New Casco in 1630, Settlement in 1633 called Casco, Part of the area called Falmouth in 1658, Destroyed by Indians in 1689, **Inc. in 1718 as Falmouth**

Farmington: Franklin Co., Settlement in 1781 called Sandy River P., **Inc. in 1794 as Farmington**

Flintstown: Cumberland Co., Settled in 1774, **See Baldwin & Sebago**

Fox Islands: Knox Co. **see North Haven & Vinalhaven**

Fox Isle: Knox Co., Settlement in 1760 called Fox Island (Originally named one of the Fox Islands by English explorer Capt. Martin Pring in1603), **Inc. in 1846 as Fox Isle, Name changed in 1847 to North Haven**

Francisborough: York Co., Trading post in 1665, Settled in 1782, **See Cornish**

Francistown: York Co., Trading post in 1665, Settled in 1782, **See Cornish**

Frankfort: Waldo Co., Settled in 1760, **Inc. in 1789 as Frankfort** (Hancock Co.), In Waldo Co. in 1827

Frankfort P.: Lincoln Co.; Settled in 1752; **See Pownalborough, Wiscasset & Dresden**

Franklin: Hancock Co., Settled in 1764 as a large part of P. # 8 and P. # 9, **Inc. in 1825 as Franklin**

Fraternity Village: Waldo Co., Settled in 1804, **See Searsmont**

Freedom: Waldo Co., Prev. to 1813 called Beaver Hill P., **Inc. in 1813 as Freedom**

Freeport: Cumberland Co., Settlement in 1700 called Harraseeket in North Yarmouth, **Inc. in 1789 as Freeport**

Freetown P. (1): Lincoln Co., Settled in 1744, **See Edgecomb**

Freetown P. (2): Kennebec Co., Settled in 1802, **See Albion and Fairfax**

Frenchboro: Hancock Co., Settled in 1812 as A V. in Long Island P., aka Frenchboro P.

Frenchboro P.: Hancock Co., **See Frenchboro**

Fryeburg: Oxford Co., Settlement in 1763 called Pigwacket, **Inc. in 1777 as Fryeburg**

Garden of Kittery: York Co., **See Eliot**

Gardiner: Kennebec Co., Settlement in 1754 in Gardinerstown P., Called Gardiner V. in Pittston in 1779, **Inc. in 1803 as Gardiner**

Gardinerstown P.: Kennebec Co., **See Gardiner & Pittston**

Garland: Penobscot Co., Settled in 1802, **Inc. in 1811 as Garland**

Georgetown: Sagadahoc Co., Settled in 1649, **Alias of Georgetown-on-Arrowsic**

Georgetown-on-Arrowsic: Sagadahoc Co., Settled in1649 in York Co., **Inc. in 1716 as Georgetown-on-Arrowsic** aka Georgetown, In Lincoln Co. in 1760, In Sagadahoc Co. in 1854

Gerry: Kennebec Co., Prev. to 1809 part of Waterford P., Settled and **Inc. in1809 as Malta, Renamed Gerry in 1821, Renamed Windsor in 1822**

Gilead: Oxford Co., Settlement in 1772 called Peabody's Patent, **Inc. in 1804 as Gilead** (Named for its "Balm of Gilead" trees)

Goldsboro: Hancock Co., Prev. to 1789 called Goldsboro P., **Inc. in 1789 as Goldsboro, Name changed to Gouldsboro in 1887**

Goldsboro P.: Hancock Co., **See Goldsboro & Gouldsboro**

Gorgeana: York Co., Settlement in 1624 called Agamenticus P., Called Bristol in 1638, **Inc. in 1642 as City of Gorgeana** (1st city in New England) by order of King Charles I, **(See York)**

Gorham: Cumberland Co., Settlement in 1736 called Gorhamtown P., **Inc. in 1764 as Gorham**

Gorhamtown P.: Cumberland Co., **See Gorham**

Gott's Island: Hancock Co., A V. in Tremont

Gouldsboro: Hancock Co., Prev. to 1789 called Goldsboro P., **Inc. in 1789 as Goldsboro, Name changed to Gouldsboro in 1887**

Gray: Cumberland Co., Settlement in 1738 called Gray, Totally destroyed and abandoned in 1745 during the French & Indian Wars, Resettled in 1751, Totally destroyed again in 1755, Resettled in1756 and called New Boston P., **Inc. in 1778 as Gray**

Great Pond: Hancock Co., Settlement in 1808 called Township # 33, Called Plantation # 33 in 1841, Called Great Pond P. in 1969, **Inc. in 1981 as Great Pond**

Great Pond P.: Hancock Co., **See Great Pond**

Great Pond Settlement: Waldo Co., **See Palermo**

Green P.: Waldo Co., **See Belmont**

Green River: Knox Co., Settlement in 1769 as Green River a V. in Rockport

Greene: Androscoggin Co., Settled in 1773 as part of Lewiston P., **Inc. in 1788 as Greene**

Green's Landing: Hancock Co., **See Stonington**

Groveville: York Co., A V. in Buxton

Hall Quarry: Hancock Co., A V. in the town of Mount Desert

Hallowell: Kennebec Co., Settled in 1762, **Inc. in 1771 as Hallowell**, **See Augusta & Harrington**

Hampden: Penobscot Co., Settlement in 1767 called Wheelersborough, **Inc. in 1794 as Hampden**

Hampton: Hancock Co., Prev. to 1831 part of Plantation # 27, 1831 Settled and **Inc. in 1831 as Hampton** aka Richards, **Name changed in 1833 to Aurora**

Hancock: Hancock Co., Settled in 1766 as part of Sullivan, Trenton and Plantation # 8, **Inc. in 1828 as Hancock**

Harlem: Kennebec Co., Settlement in 1774 called Jones P., **Inc. in 1796 as Harlem**, Became part of China in 1818

Harpswell: Cumberland Co., Settlement in 1660 called Sebascodegan a part of North Yarmouth P., **Inc. in 1758 as Harpswell District, Name changed in 1775 to Harpswell**

Harraseeket: Cumberland Co., Settled in 1700, **See Freeport**

Harrington (1): Kennebec Co., Settled in 1754, Became part of Hallowell in 1771, **Harrington split from Hallowell on 20 Feb 1797 and Inc. as Harrington, Name changed on 09 Jun 1797 to Augusta.** Note: (On 17 Jun 1797 a portion of P. # 5 in Washington Co. was split off and Inc. as Harrington.)

Harrington (2): Washington Co., Settled in 1765 as part of Plantation # 5, **Inc. in 1797 as Harrington**

Heywoodstown: Somerset Co., Settled in 1770, **See Canaan, Milburn & Skowhegan**

Hiram: Oxford Co., Settled in 1780 as part of Hiram P., **Inc. in 1814 as Hiram**

Hiram P.: Oxford Co., **See Hiram**

Holden: Penobscot Co., Prev. to 1852 a V. in Brewer, **Inc. in 1852 as Holden**

Hollis: York Co., Settled in 1781 as a V. in Little Falls P., **Inc. in 1798 as Phillipsburg, Name changed in 1812 to Hollis**

Hope: Knox Co., Prev. to 1804 called Barretstown P., **Inc. in 1804 as Hope**

Hulls Cove: Hancock Co., A V. in 1763 in town of Mount Desert, A V. in 1796 in Eden, AV. in 1918 in Bar Harbor

Huntressville: Penobscot Co., Prev. to 1837 in Township # 1, **Inc. in 1837 as Huntressville, Name changed in 1838 to Lowell**

Industry: Franklin Co., Prev. to 1803 part of Industry P., **Inc. in1803 as Industry**

Industry P.: Franklin Co., **See Industry**

Islandport: Hancock Co., Settlement in 1769 called Long Island P., **Inc. in 1857 as Islandport, Inc. repealed in 1858 and reorganized as Long Island P., See Long Island P.**

Isle au Haut: Knox Co., Named Isle au Haut in 1604 by French explorer Samuel de Champlain, A V. in Deer Isle P. in 1789 (Hancock Co.), A V. in Deer Isle in 1792 (Hancock Co.), In Knox Co. in 1860 when it was established, **Inc. in 1874 as Isle au Haut**

Isles of Shoals: York Co., Settlement of nine habitable islands began in 1623 called Isles of Shoals, All nine were **Inc. in 1661 as Appledore** by Massachusetts Bay Colony, Later, four Islands (Star, Lunging, Seavey & White) were deemed to be in Portsmouth NH (Portsmouth) while five (Appledore, Cedar, Duck, Malaga & Smuttynose) remained in **ME** (Kittery), **See Appledore**

Islesboro: Waldo Co., **Alias of Islesborough**

Islesborough: Waldo Co., Prev. to 1769 called Pitaubegwimenahanuk, Part of Long Island P. in 1769, **Inc. in 1789 as Islesborough** aka Islesboro

Jamestown: Lincoln Co., Settled in 1625, **See Bristol**

Jay: Franklin Co., Settlement in 1780 called Phipps' Canada P., **Inc. in 1795 as Jay**

Jones P.: Kennebec Co., Settled in 1774, **See China**

Joy: Waldo Co., Prev. to 1812 called Bridge's P., **Inc. in 1812 as Kingville, Renamed Joy in 1815, Renamed Montgomery in 1826, Renamed Troy in 1827**

Kennebunk: York Co., Trading post of Plymouth Colony in 1621, Settled as a V. in Wells P. in 1643, A V. in Wells in 1653, **Inc. in 1820 as Kennebunk** (Abenaki meaning: "The long cut bank")

Kennebunk Port: York Co., Settled in 1653 as part of Cape Porpus, Deserted in 1689 due to Indian attacks, Resettled in 1700, **Inc. in 1719 as Arundel, Name changed in 1821 to Kennebunk Port** aka Kennebunkport

Kennebunkport: York Co., **Alias of Kennebunk Port**

Kezar Falls: Oxford Co., Settled in 1796 as a V. in Porter

Kingville: Waldo Co., Prev. to 1812 called Bridge's P., **Inc in 1812 as Kingville, Renamed Joy in 1815, Renamed Montgomery in 1826, Renamed Troy in 1827**

Kittery: York Co., Settlement in 1623 called Piscataqua P., Called Kittery in 1635. **Inc. 20 Nov 1652 as Kittery,** Note: (1st town Inc. in what would become Maine)

Kittery Commons: York Co., Settled in 1631, **See Berwick**

Kittery North Parish: York Co., Settled in 1631, **See Berwick**

Lebanon: York Co., Settlement in 1743 called Towwah P., **Inc. in 1767 as Lebanon**

Lee P.: Waldo Co., **See Monroe**

Lemonds Cove: Knox Co., Settled in 1769, **See Rockland and East Thomaston**

Lewiston: Androscoggin Co., Settlement in 1770 called Lewiston P., Part of Greene in 1788, **Inc. in 1795 as Lewiston**

Lewiston P.: Androscoggin Co., **See Lewiston**

Liberty: Waldo Co., Settled in 1780 as part of Davistown P., Part of Montville in 1807, **Inc. in 1827 as Liberty**

Ligonia: Kennebec Co., Settlement in 1802 called Freetown P., **Inc.1804 as Fairfax, Renamed Ligonia in 1821, Renamed Albion in 1824**

Limington: York Co., Settlement in 1773 called Ossipee P., **Inc. in 1792 as Limington**

Lincoln: Penobscot Co., **Inc. in 1829 as Lincoln**

Lincolnville: Waldo Co., Settled in 1774 as part of Ducktrap and Canaan P., **Inc. in 1802 as Lincolnville**

Little Falls P.: York Co., Settled in 1781, **See Hollis and Phillipsburg**

Livermore: Androscoggin Co., Settled in 1786 as part of Livermore P., **Inc. in 1795 as Livermore** in Lincoln Co., In Kennebec Co. in 1799, In Oxford Co.in 1805, In Androscoggin Co. in 1854

Livermore Falls: Androscoggin Co., Settled in 1786 as part of Livermore P., Part of Livermore in 1799, **Inc. in 1844 as East Livermore** in Kennebec Co., In Androscoggin Co.in 1854, **Renamed Livermore Falls in 1930**

Livermore P.: Androscoggin Co., **See Livermore and East Livermore**

Long Island P.: Hancock Co., Settled in 1769, **Inc. in 1857 as Islandport, Inc. repealed in 1858 and reorganized as Long Island P., See Islandport, Islesborough & Frenchboro**

Lovell: Oxford Co., Settlement in 1777 called New Suncook P., **Inc. in 1880 as Lovell**

Lowell: Penobscot Co., Prev. to 1837 part of Township # 1, **Inc. in 1837 as Huntressville, Name changed to Lowell in 1838**

Lubec: Washington Co., Settled in 1775 as a V. in Eastport, **Inc. in 1811 as Lubec**

Lyman: York Co., Settlement in 1767 called Swanfield, **Inc. in 1780 as Coxhall, Name changed to lyman in 1803**

Machias: Washington Co., Site of a Plymouth Colony trading post in 1633 at what is now Machiasport, Later that same year, French soldiers destroyed it killing or capturing all 6 men, Machias settled in 1770, **Inc. in 1784 as Machias**

Machiasport: Washington Co., Settled in 1770 as part of Machias, A V. in Machias in 1774, **Inc. in 1826 as Machiasport**

Machigonne: Cumberland Co., Settled in 1632, **See Portland**

Maine: Penobscot Co., Settlement in 1815 called Clifton, **Inc. in 1848 as Maine, Renamed Clifton in 1849**

Majorbigwaduce: Hancock Co., Settled in **1613, See Castine and Penobscot**

Majorbigwaduce P.: Hancock Co., Settled in **1613, See Castine, Penobscot & Sedgwick**

Malaga Island: York Co., Settled in 1623, 1 of 5 Maine islands in the Isles of Shoals, **See Appledore & Isles of Shoals**

Malta: Kennebec Co., Prev. to 1809 called Waterford P., Settled in 1809 as Malta, **Inc. in 1809 as Malta, Renamed Gerry in 1821, Renamed Windsor in 1822**

Mansel: Hancock Co., Settled in 1762 as a V. in the Province of Maine, A V. in 1789 in the town of Mount Desert, **Inc. on 03 Jun 1848 as Mansel, Renamed Tremont on 07 Aug 1848**

Manset: Hancock Co., Settled in 1762 as a V. in Province of Maine, A V. in 1789 in the town of Mount Desert, A V. in 1848 in Tremont, A V. in 1905 in Southwest Harbor

Mariaville: Hancock Co., Prev. to 1836 part of Plantation # 14 and Plantation # 20, **Inc. in 1836 as Mariaville**

McKinley: Hancock Co., Settled in 1762 as a V. in the Province of Maine, **See Bass Harbor**

Mercer: Somerset Co., Prev. to 1804 part of Industry P., **Inc. in 1804 as Mercer**

Milbridge: Washington Co., Prev. to 1848 part of Harrington, **Inc. in 1848 as Milbridge**

Milburn: Somerset Co., Settlement in 1770 called Wesserunsett aka Heywoodstown, Part of Canaan in 1788, **Inc. in 1823 as Milburn**

Minot: Androscoggin Co., Settled in 1765 as part of Bakersfield P., A V. in Poland in 1795, **Inc. in 1802 as Minot**

Monmouth: Kennebec Co., Settled in 1776 as part of Wales P., **Inc. in 1792 as Monmouth**

Monroe: Waldo Co., Prev. to 1818 called Lee P., **Inc. in 1818 as Monroe**

Montgomery: Waldo Co., Prev. to 1812 called Bridge's P., **Inc. in 1812 as Kingville, Renamed Joy in 1815, Renamed Montgomery in 1826, Renamed Troy in 1827**

Montville: Waldo Co., Prev. to 1780 part of Davistown P., Settlement in 1780 called Montville, **Inc. in 1807 as Montville**

Morrill: Waldo Co., Prev. to 1855 a V. in Belmont, **Inc. in 1855 as Morrill**

Mount Desert (town of): Hancock Co., Settlement in **1613** by French Jesuits at Fernald's Point in present-day Southwest Harbor, Maine., Called Mount Desert P. in 1762 in Lincoln Co., **Inc. in 1789 as Mount Desert in Hancock Co.**

Mount Desert P.: Lincoln Co., **See Mount Desert (town of)**

Muscongus Island: York Co., A V. in Bristol

Narragansett #1: York Co., Settled in 1750, **See Buxton**

Narragansett #7: Cumberland Co., Settled in 1736, **See Gorham**

Nequasset: Sagadahoc Co., Settled in 1638, **See Woolwich**

Naskeag: Hancock Co., Settled in 1759, **See Sedgwick**

New Boston P.: Cumberland Co., Settled in 1738, **See Gray**

New Casco: Cumberland Co., A large area in 1630 around Casco Bay, This area was called Falmouth in 1658, **See Cape Elizabeth, Falmouth, Portland, South Portland & Westbrook**

New Gloucester: Cumberland Co., Settled in 1739, Abandoned in 1744 due to Indian hostilities, Resettled in 1753 by 6 families living in one stockade, **Inc. in 1774 as New Gloucester**

New Harbor: Lincoln Co., Settled in 1625 as a V. in Bristol

New Ireland: Hancock Co., **See Castine**

New Marblehead P.: Cumberland Co., Settled in 1737, **See Windham**

New Milford: Lincoln Co., Settled in 1760 as part of Pownalborough, **Inc. in 1784 as New Milford, Name changed in 1811 to Alna**

New Portland: Somerset Co., Settlement called New Portland in 1775 founded by Falmouth (present-day Portland) residents after the destruction of their town by the British Fleet on 18 Oct 1775, **Inc. in 1808 as New Portland**

New Sandwich P.: Kennebec Co., Settled in 1773, **See Wayne**

New Sharon: Franklin Co., Prev. to 1744 called Unity P., **Inc. in 1744 as New Sharon**

New Suncook P.: Oxford Co., Settled in 1777, **See Lovell**

New Vineyard: Franklin Co., Prev. to 1802 in Plantation # 2, **Inc. in 1802 as New Vineyard**

New Worcester P.: Penobscot Co., **See Orrington and Plantation # 9**

Newcastle: Lincoln Co., Settlement in 1635 called Sheepscot P., **Inc. in 1753 as Newcastle District** in York Co., In Lincoln Co. in 1760, **Inc. in 1775 as Newcastle**

Newcastle District: York Co., **See Newcastle**

Newport: Penobscot Co., Settlement in 1808 called East Pond P., **Inc. in 1814 as Newport**

Newport P.: Lincoln Co., Settled in 1762, **See Blue Hill**

Newton-on-Arrowsic: Sagadahoc Co., **See Arrowsic**

Newtown: Sagadahoc Co., Settled in 1657, **See Arrowsic**

Nobleboro: Lincoln Co., Settled in 1730, **Alias of Nobleborough**

Nobleborough: Lincoln Co., Settlement in 1730 called Walpole P., **Inc. in 1788 as Nobleborough** aka Nobleboro

Norridgewock: Somerset Co., Settlement in 1773 called Norridgewock P., **Inc. in 1788 as Norridgewock**

Norridgewock P.: Somerset Co., **See Norridgewock**

North Haven: Knox Co., Settled in 1760 as part of Vinalhaven, **Inc. in 1846 as Fox Isle, Name changed to North Haven in 1847**

North Yarmouth: Cumberland Co., Settlement in 1636 as the western part of North Yarmouth P. aka Westcustogo, "North" used due a Yarmouth already existing on Cape Cod., **Inc. in 1680 as North Yarmouth**

North Yarmouth P.: Cumberland Co., **See Harpswell & North Yarmouth**

Northeast Harbor: Hancock Co., Settlement called Northeast Harbor in 1775 as a V. in Mount Desert P., A V. in town of Mount Desert in 1789

Northport: Waldo Co., Settled in 1780 as part of Ducktrap and Canaan P. in Lincoln Co., In Hancock Co., in 1789, **Inc. in 1796 as Northport**, In Waldo Co. in 1827

Oceanville: Hancock Co., Settled in 1762 as a V. in Deer Isle P., A V. in Deer Isle in 1789, A V. in Stonington in 1897

Orland: Hancock Co., Settled in 1767 as part of Plantation # 2 EPR, **Inc. in 1800 as Orland**

Orphan Island: Settled in 1630, **See Verona Island**

Orrington: Penobscot Co., Prev. to 1788 settled as part of New Worcester P. aka Plantation # 9, **Inc. in 1788 as Orrington**

Osborn: Hancock Co., Settlement in 1840 called Township # 21, Called Osborn P. in 1923, **Inc. in 1976 as Osborn**

Osborn P.: Hancock Co., **See Osborn**

Ossipee P.: York Co., Settled in 1773, **See Limington**

Otter Creek: Hancock Co., A V. in the town of Mount Desert

Owascoag: Cumberland Co., Settled in 1631, **See Scarborough**

Owls Head: Knox Co., Settled in 1736 as part of St. George's P., Part of Thomaston in 1777, Part of South Thomaston in 1848, **Inc. in 1921 as Owls Head**

Palermo: Waldo Co., Settlement prev. to 1804 called Great Pond Settlement, **Inc. in 1804 as Palermo**

Parish of Unity: York Co., Settled in 1631, **Alias for South Berwick**

Parsonsfield: York Co., Settled in 1772, **Inc. in 1785 as Parsonsfield**

Passagassawakeag: Waldo Co., **See Belfast**

Pearsontown P.: Cumberland Co., Settled in 1752, **See Standish**

Pejepscot: Cumberland Co., Settled in 1628, **See Brunswick**

Pemaquid: Lincoln Co., Settled in 1625, **See Bristol**

Pemaquid Village: Lincoln Co., A. V. in 1765 in Bristol

Pembroke: Washington Co., Settled in 1774 as part of Dennysville, **Inc. in 1832 as Pembroke**

Penobscot: Hancock Co., Settlement in 1765 called Majorbigwaduce a part of Township # 3 EPR, **Inc. in 1787 as Penobscot**

Penobscot Island: Settled in 1630, **See Verona Island**

Pentagoët: Hancock Co., **See Castine**

Pepperrellborough: York Co., Settlement and **Inc. in 1762 as Pepperrellborough District, Name changed to Pepperrellborough in 1775, Name changed to Saco in 1805**

Phillipsburg: York Co., Settled in 1781 as part of Little Falls P., **Inc. in 1798 as Phillipsburg, Name changed to Hollis in 1812**

Phillipstown P.: York Co., Settled in 1739, **See Sanford**

Phipps' Canada P.: Franklin Co., Settled in 1780, **See Jay**

Phippsburg: Sagadahoc Co., Settled in 1649 as part of Gorges Patent, Part of Georgetown P. in 1779, **Inc. in 1814 as Phippsburg** (Lincoln Co.), In Sagadahoc Co. in 1854

Pigwacket: Oxford Co., Settled in 1763, **See Fryeburg**

Piscatuqua P.: York Co., **See Kittery and Berwick**

Pitaubegwimenahanuk (Easy for you to say!): Waldo Co., **See Islesborough**

Pittston: Kennebec Co., Prev. to 1779 part of Gardinerstown P., **Inc. in 1779 as Pittston**

Plantation No. 1: **See Bucksport and Trenton**

Plantation No. 2 EUR: **See Sullivan and New Vineyard**

Plantation No. 2 EPR: **See Orland**

Plantation No. 3: **See Charlotte**

Plantation No. 4: **See Steuben**

Plantation No. 5: **See Harrington and Cherryfield**

Plantation No. 6: **See Addison**

Plantation No. 8: **See Franklin, Hancock and Eastport**

Plantation No. 9 aka New Worcester P.: **See Orrington, Franklin and Trescott**

Plantation No. 10: **See Edmunds**

Plantation No. 11: **See Cutler**

Plantation No. 14: **See Waltham and Mariaville**

Plantation No. 18: **See East Machias**

Plantation No. 20: **See Mariaville and Amherst**

Plantation No. 26: **See Amherst**

Plantation No. 27: **See Hampton and Aurora**

Plantation No. 33: **See Great Pond**

Poland: Androscoggin Co., Settlement in 1765 called Bakersfield P., **Inc. in 1795 as Poland**

Pondstown P.: Kennebec Co., **See Winthrop**

Port Watson: Hancock Co., Settlement in 1759 called Naskeag, Part of Sedgwick in 1789, **Inc. on 09 Jul 1849 as Port Watson, Renamed Brooklin on 23 Jul 1849**

Porter: Oxford Co., Settlement in 1796 called Porterfield P., **Inc. in 1807 as Porter**

Porterfield P.: Oxford Co., **See Porter**

Portland: Cumberland Co., Settlement in 1632 called Machigonne aka Casco, Part of Falmouth in 1658, **Inc. in 1786 as Portland**

Pownalborough: Lincoln Co., Settlement in 1752 called Frankfort P., **Inc. in 1760 as Pownalborough**

Pretty Marsh: Hancock Co., A V. in town of Mount Desert

Prospect: Waldo Co., Settlement in1759 called Stockton, **Inc. in 1794 as Prospect, Name changed in 1857 to Stockton, Name changed in 1889 to Stockton Springs**

Prospect Harbor: Hancock Co., A V. in Gouldsboro

Purpooduc: Cumberland Co., Settled in 1630 in the area called New Casco, **See Cape Elizabeth & South Portland**

Quantabacook: Waldo Co., **See Searsmont**

Ragged Arse Island, Knox Co., **See Criehaven Island**

Raymond: Cumberland Co., Settlement in 1779 called Raymondtown aka Raymond P., **Inc. in 1803 as Raymond**

Raymond P.: Cumberland Co., **See Raymond**

Raymondtown: Cumberland Co., **See Raymond**

Richards: Hancock Co., **See Aurora**

Richmond: Sagadahoc Co., Settled in 1725 as part of Bowdoinham, **Inc. in 1823 as Richmond**

Riverton: Cumberland Co., Settled in 1633, A neighborhood in Westbrook

Rockland: Knox Co., Settlement in 1769 called Lemond's Cove part of St Georges P., Called Shore Village in 1777 in Thomaston, **Inc. in 1848 as East Thomaston, Name changed in 1850 to Rockland**

Rockport: Knox Co., Settled in 1769 as part of Megunicook P., Part of Camden in 1791, Called Green River V. in 1852 in Camden, **Inc. in 1891 as Rockport**

Round Pond: Lincoln Co., Settled in 1765 as a V. in Bristol

Saccarappa: Cumberland Co., Settled in 1633 as a V. in Falmouth, **See Westbrook**

Saco (1): York Co., Settled in 1631 as part of Winter Harbor (1), **Inc. in 1653 as Saco**, Destroyed by fire during King William's War in 1690 and abandoned

Saco (2): York Co., The prior town of Saco was rebuilt and resettled by 1718 as a part of Biddeford, **Inc. in 1762 as Pepperrellborough District, Name changed in 1775 to Pepperrellborough, Name changed in 1805 to Saco**

St George: Knox Co., Settled in 1736 as part of St George's P., Called St George in 1789 a V. in Cushing, **Inc. in 1803 as St George**

St George's P.: Knox Co., **See Cushing, East Thomaston, Rockland, St George, Thomaston, and Warren**

Salisbury Cove: Hancock Co., A V. in Mount Desert in1763, A V. in Eden in 1796, A V. in Bar Harbor in 1918

Salmon Falls: York Co., A V. in Buxton

Sandy River P.: Franklin Co., **See Farmington**

Sanford: York Co., Settled in 1739 as part of Phillipstown P., **Inc. in 1768 as Sanford**

Sargentville: Hancock Co., Settled in 1739 as a V. in Sedgwick

Sawacook: Sagadahoc Co., **See Topsham**

Scarborough: Cumberland Co., Prev. to 1631 called Owascoag, Settlement in 1631 called Blue Point, **Inc. in 1658 as Scarborough**

Seal Cove: Hancock Co., Settled in 1762 as a V. in Tremont

Seal Harbor: Hancock Co., A V. in town of Mount Desert

Searsmont: Waldo Co., Prev. to 1804 called Quantabacook, Settlement in 1804 called Fraternity Village, **Inc. in 1814 as Searsmont**

Searsport: Waldo Co., Settled in 1670, **Inc. in 1845 as Searsport** from parts of Prospect & Belfast

Sebago: Cumberland Co., Settlement in 1774 called Flintstown, Part of Baldwin in 1802, **Inc. in 1826 as Sebago**

Sebascodegan: Cumberland Co., Settled in 1660, **See Harpswell**

Sedgwick: Hancock Co., Settlement in 1759 called Naskeag (York Co.), Called Naskeag in 1760 (Lincoln Co.), Called Naskeag V. in Majorbigwaduce P. in 1761 (Lincoln Co.), **Inc. in 1789 as Sedgwick** (Hancock Co.)

Shapleigh: York Co., Settled in 1776, **Inc. in 1785 as Shapleigh**

Sheepscot P.: Lincoln Co., Settled in 1635, **See Newcastle**

Shore Village: Knox Co., Settled in 1769, **See East Thomaston & Rockland**

Skowhegan: Somerset Co., Settlement in 1770 called Wesserunsett aka Heywoodstown, Part of Canaan in 1773, **Inc. in 1823 as Milburn, Name changed in 1836 to Skowhegan**

Smutty-Nose Island: York Co., 1 of 5 Maine islands in the Isles of Shoals in 1623, **See Appledore & Isles of Shoals**

Somesville: Hancock Co., Settled in 1762 by Capt. Abraham and Hannah (Herrick) Somes as a V. in Mount Desert P., A V. in town of Mount Desert in 1789, Note (First village on Mount Desert Island)

South Berwick: York Co., Settlement in 1631 as part of Kittery called North Parish aka Parish of Unity, Called South Berwick V. in Berwick in 1713, **Inc. in 1814 as South Berwick**

South Deer Isle: Hancock Co., A V. in Deer Isle

South Portland: Cumberland Co., Settled as part of Purpoodoc in 1630, Part of Cape Elizabeth in 1785, **Inc. in 1895 as South Portland**

South Thomaston: Knox Co., Settled in 1763 as part of Thomaston, **Inc. in 1848 as South Thomaston**

Southport: Lincoln Co., Settlement in 1623 as a fishing village called Cape Newagen Island, **Inc. in 1842 as Southport**

Southwest Harbor: Hancock Co., Settled about 1763 as part of Mount Desert P. (Lincoln Co.), Called Southwest Harbor a V. in the town of Mount Desert (Hancock Co.) in 1789, Called Southwest Harbor a V. in Tremont in 1848, **Inc. in 1905 as Southwest Harbor**

Springfield: Penobscot Co., **Inc. in 1834 as Springfield**

Spurwink: Cumberland Co., Settled in 1630 as a V. on the Spurwink River in Purpooduc, A V. in Cape Elizabeth in 1665

Standish: Cumberland Co., Settlement in 1752 called Pearsontown P., **Inc. in 1785 as Standish**

Sterlingtown P.: Knox Co., Settlement in 1774 called Taylor Town, Called Sterlingtown P. in 1786, **See Union**

Steuben: Washington Co., Prev. to 1795 part of Plantation # 4, **Inc. in 1795 as Steuben**

Stockton: Waldo Co., Settlement in 1759 called Stockton, **Inc. in 1794 as Prospect, Name changed in 1857 to Stockton, Name changed in 1889 to Stockton Springs**

Stockton Springs: Waldo Co., Settlement in 1759 called Stockton, **Inc. in 1794 as Prospect, Name changed in 1857 to Stockton, Name changed in 1889 to Stockton Springs**

Stonington: Hancock Co., Settled in 1762 as part of Deer Isle P. (Lincoln Co.), Part of Deer Isle (Hancock Co.) in 1789, Called Green's landing in 1800, **Inc. in 1897 as Stonington**

Stroudwater: Cumberland Co., Settlement in 1633 called Saccarappa a V. in Falmouth, **Inc. in 1814 as Stroudwater, Name changed to Westbrook in 1814**

Sudbury-Canada P.: Oxford Co., Settled in 1774, **See Bethel**

Sullivan: Hancock Co., Prev. to 1789 part of Plantation # 2 EUR, **Inc. in 1789 as Sullivan**

Sunset: Hancock Co., A V. in Deer Isle

Sunshine: Hancock Co., A V. in Deer Isle

Surry: Hancock Co., Settlement in 1762 called Township # 6 EPR, **Inc. in 1803 as Surry**

Swanfield: York Co., Settled in 1767, **See Coxhall and Lyman**

Swans Island: Hancock Co., Settlement in 1791 called Swans Island P., **Inc. in 1897 as Swans Island**

Swans Island P.: Hancock Co., **See Swans Island**

Sylvester-Canada: Androsgoggin Co., Settled in 1772, **See Turner**

Taylor Town: Knox Co., Settlement in 1774 called Taylor Town, Called Sterlingtown P. in 1786, **See Union**

Temple: Franklin Co., Settled in 1796, **Inc. in 1803 as Temple**

Thomaston: Knox Co., Settlement in 1736 as part of St Georges P., **Inc. in 1777 as Thomaston**

Topsham: Sagadahoc Co., Settlement in 1632 called Sawacook, Called Topsham in 1717, **Inc. in 1764 as Topsham**

Town Hill: Hancock Co., A V. in Bar Harbor

Townsend: Lincoln Co., Settlement in 1730 called Townsend, **Inc. in 1764 as Townsend, Renamed Boothbay in 1842**

Township # 1: Penobscot Co., **See Huntressville and Lowell**

Township # 3 EPR: Hancock Co., **See Castine and Penobscot**

Township # 4 EPR: Hancock Co., Settled in 1760, **See Steuben and Bradley**

Township # 6 EPR: Hancock Co., **See Surry**

Township # 12: Washington Co., Settled in 1770, **See Columbia & Whiting**

Township # 13: Washington Co., Settled in 1770, **See Columbia Falls**

Township # 21: Hancock Co., **See Osborn**

Township # 23: Washington Co., Settled in 1770, **See Centreville**

Township # 33: Hancock Co., **See Great Pond**

Towwah P.: York Co., Settled in 1743, **See Lebanon**

Tremont: Hancock Co., Settled in 1762 in Province of Maine, Called Tremont in the town of Mount Desert in 1789, **Inc. 03 Jun 1848 as Mansel, Renamed Tremont on 07 Aug 1848**

Trenton: Hancock Co., Prev. to 1789 called Plantation # 1, **Inc. in 1789 as Trenton**

Troy: Waldo Co., Prev. to 1812 called Bridge's P., **Inc. in 1812 as Kingville, Renamed Joy in 1815, Renamed Montgomery in 1826, Renamed Troy in 1827**

Turner: Androsgoggin Co., Settlement in 1772 called Sylvester-Canada, **Inc. in 1786 as Turner**

Twenty-five Mile Pond P.: Waldo Co., **See Unity**

Union: Knox Co., Settlement in 1774 called Taylor Town, Called Sterlingtown P. on 03 May 1786, **Inc. as Union on 20 Oct 1786**

Unity: Waldo Co., Prev. to 1804 known as Twenty-five Mile Pond P., **Inc. in 1804 as Unity**

Unity P.: Franklin Co., **See New Sharon**

Vassallborough: Kennebec Co., **Inc. in 1771 as Vassallborough**

Verona: Hancock Co., Settled in 1630, **Inc. in 1861 as Verona, See Verona Island**

Verona Island: Hancock Co., Settlement in 1630 called Penobscot Island, Called Orphan Island in 1806, Called Wetmore Island P. in 1839, **Inc. in 1861 as Verona, Renamed Verona Island in 2004**

Vinalhaven: Knox Co., Prev. to 1766 called one of the Fox Islands (Originally named Fox Islands by English explorer Capt. Martin Pring in1603), Settlement called Vinalhaven in 1766, **Inc. in 1789 as Vinalhaven**

Waldo: Waldo Co., Settlement in 1811 called Waldo Patent, **Inc. in 1845 as Waldo** (Where's Waldo? About 4 miles northwest of Belfast)

Waldo Patent: Waldo Co., **See Waldo**

Waldoboro: Lincoln Co., **Alias of Waldoborough**

Waldoborough: Lincoln Co., Settlement in 1733 called Broad Bay, **Inc. in 1773 as Waldoborough** aka Waldoboro

Wales P.: Kennebec Co., Settled in 1776, **See Monmouth**

Walpole P.: Lincoln Co., Settled in 1730, **See Nobleborough**

Waltham: Hancock Co., Prev. to 1833 called Plantation # 14, **Inc. in 1833 as Waltham**

Warren: Knox Co., Settled in 1736 as the western part of Georges P., **Inc. in 1776 as Warren**

Washington P.: Kennebec Co., **See Belgrade**

Waterford: Oxford Co., Settled in 1777, **Inc. in 1797 as Waterford**

Waterford P.: Kennebec Co., **See Windsor**

Waterville: Kennebec Co., Settled as a part of Winslow, **Inc. in 1802 as Waterville, Inc. in 1888 as City of Waterville**

Wayne: Kennebec Co., Prev. to 1798 called New Sandwich P., **Inc. in 1798 as Wayne**

Wells: York Co., Settlement in 1643 called Wells P., **Inc. in 1653 as Wells** Note: (3rd town Inc. in what would become Maine)

Wells P.: York Co., **See Wells**

Wesserunsett: Somerset Co., Settled in 1770, **See Canaan, Milburn & Skowhegan**

West Bowdoinham P.: Sagadahoc Co., Settled in 1770, **See Bowdoin**

West Buxton: York Co., Settled in 1750 as a V. in Buxton

West Gardiner: Kennebec Co., Settled in 1754, **Inc. in 1803 as West Gardiner**

West Tremont: Hancock Co., Settled about 1763 as a V. in Tremont

Westbrook: Cumberland Co., Settlement in 1633 called Saccarappa in the area called New Casco, Still called Saccarappa in 1658 in the area called Falmouth, **Inc. in 1814 as Stroudwater, Name changed that same year (1814) to Westbrook**

Westcustogo: Cumberland Co., **See North Yarmouth & Yarmouth**

Wetmore Island P.: Hancock Co., **See Verona Island**

Wheelersborough: Penobscot Co., **See Hampden**

Whiting: Washington Co., Prev. to 1825 called Plantation # 12, **Inc. in 1825 as Whiting**

Windham: Cumberland Co., Settlement in 1737 called New Marblehead P., **Inc. in 1762 as Windham**

Windsor: Kennebec Co., Prev. to 1809 called New Waterford P., **Inc. in 1809 as Malta, Renamed Gerry in 1821, Renamed Windsor in 1822**

Winslow: Kennebec Co., Settled in 1760 around Fort Halifax (Built in 1754), **Inc. in 1771 as Winslow**

Winter Harbor (1): York Co., Settled in 1631, **See Saco and Biddeford**

Winter Harbor (2): Hancock Co., Prev. to 1895 a V. in Gouldsboro, **Inc. in 1895 as Winter Harbor**

Winterport: Waldo Co., Settled in 1766 as part of Frankfort, **Inc. in 1860 as Winterport, Note:** (Named Winterport as this Penobscot R. port usually stays ice-free in the winter.)

Winthrop: Kennebec Co., Prev. to 1771 called Pondstown P., **Inc. in 1771 as Winthrop**

Wiscasset: Lincoln Co., Settled in 1752 as part of Frankfort P., Part of Pownalborough in 1760, **Inc. in 1802 as Wiscasset**

Woolwich: Sagadahoc Co., Settlement in 1638 called Nequasset, A V. in Georgetown in 1725, **Inc. in 1759 as Woolwich District, Name changed in 1775 to Woolwich**

Yarmouth: Cumberland Co., Settlement in 1636 as the eastern part of North Yarmouth P. aka Westcustogo, Abandoned due to the Indian wars in 1676, Resettled as the eastern part of N. Yarmouth in 1680, Once more abandoned in 1688 due to the Indian wars and not resettled until 1722, **Inc. in 1849 as Yarmouth**

York: York Co., Settlement in 1624 as part of Agamenticus P., Agamenticus P. called Bristol in 1638, In 1642 York was part of newly-incorporated "City of Gorgeana" (1st City in New England), **Inc. 22 Nov 1652 as York** Note: (2nd town Inc. in what would become Maine. Kittery, the 1st town in Maine, was Inc. two days prior on 20 Nov 1652.)

CHAPTER III
MASSACHUSETTS

1635 Massachusetts General Court Law regarding settlements:
"...no home was to be above a half a mile away from the Meeting House."
(Excluded mill-houses and preexisting homes)

Colonial Era Events in Massachusetts

1620: **Plymouth Colony Settled;** The *Mayflower* arrives with 102 passengers and the Plymouth Colony, aka New Plymouth Colony or Plymouth Bay Colony, is established.

1623: **Nantasket Beach Colony;** A permanent fishing village called the Nantasket Beach Colony, aka Cape Ann Colony, is permanently established by the Dorchester Company at Cape Ann that would later become Gloucester

1625: **First European Settlement;** The Rev. William Blaxton (aka Blackstone) of the Anglican Church immigrated to the New World in 1623. About 1625, he was the first settler on a large tract on what would become Boston Common and Beacon Hill. In 1630, he invited residents of Charlestown to move to his land where they could find the fresh water they wanted. His invited guests soon informed him that his land was owned by the Massachusetts Bay Colony. The Colony then deeded him 50 acres, which he promptly sold back to the Colony. Feeling threatened by his Anglican support of the Church of England, the intolerant puritans burned down his home in 1635. He then moved 35 miles south to a hill overlooking what is now the Blackstone River and became the first settler of what would become Rhode Island. There is a monument marking his grave in Cumberland Rhode Island.

1626: **Naumkeag Settled;** Called Salem in 1629, Naumkeag was settled by many residents of the failed Nantasket Beach Colony

1630: **Massachusetts Bay Colony (MBC);** The "Great Migration" begins with the the establishment of a second Colony to augment the Plymouth Colony. It started in 1630 with about 700 immigrants arriving with the Winthrop Fleet. The European population in the New World grew from a few missionaries and fisherman prior to the *Mayflower* to about 4,600 by 1630 and 22,000 by 1640.

1642: **School Act of Massachusetts;** This law required that all children be taught reading, citizenship and religion.

1643: Massachusetts Counties Established; Excluding the Plymouth Colony, MBC was organized into four counties with towns and villages as follows:

ESSEX	MIDDLESEX	NORFOLK	SUFFOLK
Cochichawicke	Cambridge	Dover	Boston
Gloucester	Charlestown	Exeter	Braintree
Ipswich	Concord	Hampton	Dedham
Lynn	Medford	Haverhill	Dorchester
Newbury	Reading	Salisbury	Hingham
Rowley	Sudbury	Strawberry Banke	Roxbury
Salem	Watertown		Weymouth
Wenham	Wayland		
	Woburn		

1652: York County; York County was added to above initial four counties by MBC and would be transferred to the new State of Maine in 1820

1662: Hampshire County; Organized by MBC

1674: Devonshire County; Located between the Kennebec River and Penobscot Bay in "Maine", all of its settlements had been abandoned by 1676 due to King Philip's War and Devonshire County ceased to exist except on paper.

1679: Province of New Hampshire; A new Province of New Hampshire, still governed by MBC, was formed as Norfolk County, one of the original four counties, was abolished. MBC retained some territory on the North bank of the Merrimack River (Salisbury and Haverhill) that were absorbed into Essex County. The Province of New Hampshire assumed authority over the remaining towns from Norfolk County.

1685: Barnstable, Bristol and Plymouth Counties; Plymouth Colony, feeling uninvited to the party, divides its territory into three counties.

1686: Dominion of New England; All of the America Colonies from the Delaware River to Penobscot Bay in Maine were declared one entity, Dominion of New England, by King James II. From the outset, there was mass resistance to that concept because the colonists resented being stripped of rights by anyone, let alone a King who had strong ties to the Catholic Church.

1689: Dominion of New England Collapses; After King James II was overthrown in December 1688, the Colonies ousted Dominion officials and reverted to their previous structures and authorities.

1691: Province of Massachusetts Bay (PMB); Plymouth and Massachusetts Bay Colonies merge to form the Province of Massachusetts Bay.

1695: Dukes and Nantucket Counties; PMB acquires the island counties of Dukes and Nautucket (Renamed Nantucket by PMB) from New York

1731: Worcester County Organized; Taking parts of Middlesex, Suffolk and Hampshire Counties,

PMB formed the new county of Worcester.

1746: **Some PMB territory awarded to Rhode Island (RI);** The Court awarded the PMB towns and villages of Barrington, Sowams, Bristol, East Pawtucket and West Pawtucket to RI who formed a new Bristol County, RI with those communities. Also, the PMB towns of Tiverton and Little Compton joined the preexisting Newport County, RI. This action resolved all existing border disputes between PMB and RI.

1749: **Massachusetts towns ceded to Connecticut (CT);** PMB towns of Enfield, Somers, Suffield and Woodstock were ceded to CT resolving all border disputes between PMB and CT.

1760: **Cumberland and Lincoln Counties Established by PMB;** Transferred to the new State of Maine in 1820.

1761: **Berkshire County Established by PMB**

1788: **Massachusetts (MA) Statehood;** Massachusetts became the 6th of the original 13 States to ratify the Constitution.

1789: **Hancock and Washington Counties Established by MA;** Transferred to new State of Maine in 1820

1793: **"New" Norfolk County. Established by MA;** "Old" Norfolk Co. had been abolished in 1679

1799: **Kennebec County Established by MA;** Transferred to new State of Maine in 1820

1805: **Oxford County Established by MA;** Transferred to new State of Maine in 1820

1809: **Somerset County Established by MA;** Transferred to new State of Maine in 1820

1811: **Franklin County Established by MA**

1812: **Hampden County Established by MA**

1816: **Penobscot County Established by MA;** Transferred to new State of Maine in 1820

1820: **Devonshire County Abandoned;** When the MA District of Maine became the State of Maine in 1820, in addition to the transfer of those counties noted above, MA abandoned any claim it might have had to the ill-fated Devonshire County.

MASSACHUSETTS SETTLEMENTS

Populated Place

Abington: Plymouth Co., Settlement in 1668 called Manamooskeagin (Land of many beavers), Called

Abington V. in 1706, **Inc. in 1712 as Abington**

Acton: Middlesex Co., Settled in 1639 as part of Concord, **Inc. in 1735 as Acton**

Acushnet: Bristol Co., Settlement in 1659 as a V. in Dartmouth, A V. in New Bedford in 1787, A V. in Fairhaven in 1812, **Inc. in 1860 as Acushnet**

Agamenticus: Gorges Patent, Settlement in 1624 called Agamenticus, **See Georgeana**

Agawam: Essex Co., Settled in 1630, **See Ipswich and Wareham**

Agawam P. Hampshire Co., **See Springfield**

Amesbury: Essex Co., Called Merrimac P. in 1638, Settlement called Newtown V. in Salisbury in 1642, In "Old" Norfolk Co. in 1643, **Inc. in 1668 as Amesbury in "Old" Norfolk Co.,** In Essex Co. in 1679 when "Old" Norfolk Co. was abolished

Andover: Essex Co., Settlement in 1641 called Cochichawicke, **Inc. in 1646 as Andover**

Aquinnah: Dukes Co., Settlement in 1669 called Aquinnah aka Gay Head, A V. in Chilmark in 1694, **Inc. in 1870 as Gay Head, Renamed Aquinnah in 1997**

Arlington: Middlesex Co., Settlement in 1635 Called Menotomy a V. in Cambridge, Called Menotomy a V. in West Cambridge in 1807, **Inc. in 1867 as Arlington** (Named for National Cemetery)

Ashburnham: Worcester Co., Settlement in 1736 called Plantation of Dorchester-Canada, **Inc. in 1765 as Ashburnham**

Ashby: Middlesex Co., Settled in 1676, **Inc. in 1767 as Ashby**

Ashfield: Franklin Co., Settlement in 1743 called Huntstown, **Inc. in 1765 as Ashfield**

Ashland: Middlesex Co., Settlement in 1750 called Unionville, **Inc. in 1846 as Ashland**

Athol: Worcester Co., Settlement in 1735 called Pequoiag, **Inc. in 1762 as Athol**

Attleboro: Bristol Co., Settled in 1634 as part of Rehoboth, **Inc. in 1694 as Attleborough, Renamed Attleboro in 1914**

Attleborough: Bristol Co., **See Attleboro**

Auburn: Worcester Co., Settlement in 1714 called South Parish of Worcester, **Inc. in 1778 as Ward, Name changed to Auburn in 1837,** Note: P.O. Complained that Ward was too similar to Ware so it had to be changed.)

Augumtoocooke: Middlesex Co., **See Dracut**

Avon: Norfolk Co., Settlement in 1713 called Avon a V. in Stoughton, **Inc. in 1888 as Avon**

Awassamog: Middlesex Co., Settlement in 1659 as the first Nipmuc Praying Indian V., **See Holliston**

Barecove: Plymouth Co., Settled in 1633, **See Hingham**

Barnstable: Barnstable Co., Settled in 1638, **Inc. in 1639 as Barnstable**

Barre: Worcester Co., Settlement in 1720 called Northwest District of Rutland, **Inc. in 1774 as Hutchinson, Name changed in 1776 to Barre**

Barrington: Bristol Co., Settled in 1667 as part of Swansea, **Inc. in 1717 as Barrington, Ceded in 1747 to RI**

Bedford: Middlesex Co., Settled in 1640 as part of Concord, Part of Concord and Billerica in 1655, **Inc. in 1729 as Bedford**

Bellingham: Norfolk Co., Settlement in 1713 called Westham (Contraction of West Dedham) in Suffolk Co., **Inc. in 1719 as Bellingham** in Suffolk Co., In "New" Norfolk Co. when it was formed in 1793

Berkley: Bristol Co., Settled in 1638 as part of Dighton V. and Taunton, **Inc. in 1735 as Berkley**

Berlin: Worcester Co., Settled in 1665, Called District of Berlin a part of Marlborough and Bolton in 1784, **Inc. in 1812 as Berlin**

Bernardston: Franklin Co., Prev. to 1762 called Falltown P. aka Falls Flight, **Inc. in 1762 as Bernardston**

Beverly: Essex Co., Settled in 1626 as part of Salem, **Inc. in 1668 as Beverly**

Billerica: Middlesex Co., Settlement in 1652 called Shawshin, later a Praying Indian V., **Inc. in 1655**

as Billerica

Billingsgate: Barnstable Co., Prev to 1651 a fishing V. on Cape Cod, **See Wellfleet**

Black Horse Village: Middlesex Co., Settled in 1640, **See Winchester**

Boggestow: Middlesex Co., Settled in 1652, **See Sherborn**

Bolton: Worcester Co., Settled in 1682 as part of Lancaster, **Inc. in 1738 as Bolton**

Boston: Suffolk Co., Prev. to 1630 called Trimountaine, Settled in 1630 by Puritans from Charlestown V. seeking a source of fresh water, **Inc. in 1630 as Boston, Inc. in 1822 as City of Boston**

Bourne: Barnstable Co., Settled in 1640 as part of Sandwich, **Inc. in 1884 as Bourne**

Boxboro: Middlesex Co., **Alias of Boxborough**

Boxborough: Middlesex Co., Sett;ed in 1680, **Inc. in 1783 as Boxborough aka Boxboro**

Boxford: Essex Co., Settled in 1646 as part of Rowley, **Inc. in 1685 as Boxford**

Boylston: WorcesterCo., Settled in 1726, **Inc. in 1786 as Boylston**

Bradford: Essex Co., Settled in 1639 as part of Rowley, **Inc. in 1668 as Bradford, Annexed in 1897 by Haverhill**

Braintree (Town of): Norfolk Co., Settlement in 1625 called Braintree, In Suffolk Co. in 1634, **Inc. in 1640 as "Town of Braintree"**, In the "New" Norfolk Co. in 1793, **Inc. in 2008 as City of Braintree**

Brewster: Barnstable Co., Settled in 1656 as part of Yarmouth, Part of Harwich in 1694, **Inc. in 1803 as Brewster**

Bridgewater: Plymouth Co., Settled in 1650 as part of Duxbury, **Inc. in 1656 as Bridgewater**

Brighton: Middlesex Co., Settled in 1630 as part of Watertown, Part of New Towne in 1634, Part of Cambridge in 1636, Called Little Cambridge in 1796, **Inc. in 1807 as Brighton**

Brimfield: Hampden Co., Settled in 1706, **Inc. in 1731 as Brimfield**

Bristol (1): York Co., **See Georgeana**

Bristol (2): Bristol Co., Settled in 1680 as Bristol V. in Plymouth Co., Called Bristol V. in Bristol Co. in 1685, Ceded to **RI** in 1747

Brocton: Plymouth Co., Settled in 1700, **Inc. in 1821 as Brocton**

Brookfield: Worcester Co., Settled in 1660 as part of Quaborg P., Part of Bridgewater in 1700, **Inc. in 1718 as Brookfield**

Brookline: Norfolk Co., Settlement in 1638 called Muddy River a V. in Boston, A V. in Woburn in 1641, **Inc. in 1705 as Brookline,** In the "New" Norfolk Co. in 1793

Burlington: Middlesex Co., Settled in 1641, **Inc. in 1799 as Burlington**

Byfield: Essex Co., A V. in Newbury

Cambridge: Middlesex Co., Settlement in 1630 called Newe Towne, **Inc. in 1636 as Cambridge**

Cambridge Farms: Middlesex Co., Settled in 1642, **See Lexington**

Cambridge Village: Middlesex Co., Settled in 1630 as part of Newe Towne V., Part of Cambridge in 1636, **Inc. in 1688 as Cambridge Village, See Newton**

Canton: Norfolk Co., Settled in 1713 as a V. in Stoughton, **Inc. in 1797 as Canton** in the "New" Norfolk Co.

Cape Ann: Essex Co., Settled in 1623, **See Gloucester and Rockport**

Carlisle: Middlesex Co., Settled in 1651 as part of Acton, Billerica, Chelmsford and Concord, Organized as a District of Concord in 1780, **Inc. in 1805 as Carlisle**

Carver: Plymouth Co., Prev. to 1660 called Wankinquag, Settled in 1660 as part of Plympton V. in Plymouth, Called Western Parish a V. in Plymouth in 1662, Called Carver a V. in Plymouth in 1707, **Inc. in 1790 as Carver**

Centerville: Barnstable Co., Prev. to 1637, called Chequaquet (Pleasant Harbor), Settled in 1637 as a V. in Barnstable

Charlestown: Suffolk Co., Settlement in 1624 called Mishawaum, Called Charlestowne V. in 1628, Called Charlestown a V. in Boston in 1630, **Inc. in 1847 as Charlestown**, Annexed by Boston in 1874. Note: (This area was called Charlestown for 219 years before it was Inc. as the town of Charlestown in 1847 and had been a town for only 27 years when it was annexed by Boston.

Charlestown Beyond the Neck: Middlesex Co., Settlement in anticipation of the Winthrop Fleet in 1629 called Charlestown Beyond the Neck, **See Somerville**

Charlestowne V.: Suffolk Co., **See Charlestown**

Chatham: Barnstable Co., Prev. to 1656 called Monomoit a "Constablewick" (Jurisdiction or district of a constable), Settled in1656, A V. in Rehoboth in 1665, **Inc. in 1712 as Chatham**

Chebacco Parish: Essex Co., Settled in 1634 as a V. in Ipswich, **Inc. in 1819 as Essex**

Chelmsford: Middlesex Co., Settled in 1633 by families from Woburn and Concord, **Inc. in 1655 as Chelmsford**

Chelsea: Suffolk Co., Settlement in 1624 called Winnisimmet, Called Chelsea a V. in Boston in 1632, Along with other Boston Villages of Pullen Poynt and Rumney Marsh **Inc. in 1739 as Chelsea**

Chequaquet: Barnstable Co., **See Centerville**

Chicopee: Hampden Co., Settled in 1640 as part of Springfield, **Inc. in 1848 as Chicopee**

Chicopee Falls: Hampden Co., Settled in 1660 as a V. in Springfield

Chilmark: Dukes Co., Settled in 1660 as part of Tisbury, **Inc. in 1694 as Chilmark**

Clayton: Berkshire Co., A V. in New Marlborough

Cochichawicke: Essex Co., Settled in 1641 as Cochichawicke V., **See Andover**

Cohannett: Bristol Co., Settled in 1637 as Cohannett V., **See Taunton**

Cohasset: Norfolk Co., Settled in 1647 as part of Hingham, A V. in Hingham in 1670, **Inc. in   1775 as Cohasset** in Suffolk Co., In "New" Norfolk Co. in 1793

Colchester: Essex Co., Settled in 1637 as Colchester V., **Inc. in Sep 1639 as Colchester, Renamed Salisbury in Oct 1639**

Colrain: Franklin Co., Settlement in 1735 called Boston Township # 2, **Inc. in 1761 as Colrain aka Colraine**

Concord: Middlesex Co., Prev. to 1635 called Musketaquid, Settled in 1635 as Concord V., **Inc. in 1635 as Concord**

Contentment: Norfolk Co., Settled in 1635 as Contentment V., **See Dedham**

Crocksett: Worcester Co., Settled in 1720 as Second Parish of Lancaster aka Crocksett, **See Sterling**

Danvers: Essex Co., Settlement in 1626 called Salem Village, Called Salem Village a V. in Salem in 1629, Called Danvers a V. in Salem in 1752, **Inc. in 1757 as Danvers**

Dartmouth: Bristol Co., Settlement in 1650 by Plymouth Quakers called Dartmouth, **Inc. in 1664 as Dartmouth,** Dartmouth villages of New Bedford, Acushnet, and Fairhaven secede from Dartmouth and Inc. as New Bedford in 1787.

Dedham: Norfolk Co., Settlement in 1635 called Contentment, **Inc. in 1636 as Dedham,** In Suffolk Co. in 1643, In "New" Norfolk Co. when it was formed in 1793 designated as its County Seat

Deerfield: Franklin Co., Prev. to 1673 called Pocumtuck, Settlement in 1673 called Deerfield V., Site of "Battle of Bloody Brook" massacre in 1675, **Inc. in 1677 as Deerfield,** Site of "Raid on Deerfield" massacre in 1704

Deerfield Northwest: Franklin Co., Settlement in 1756 as Deerfield Northwest a V. in Deerfield, **See Shelburne**

Dennis: Barnstable Co., Settled in 1639 as part of Yarmouth, **Inc. in 1793 as Dennis**

Dighton: Bristol Co., Settled in 1637 as part of Cohannett V., Part of Taunton in 1639, A V. in Taunton in 1672, **Inc. in 1712 as Dighton**

District of Berlin: Worcester Co., Settled in 1665, **See Berlin**

District of Dedham: Norfolk Co., Settled in 1640, **Inc. in 1784 as District of Dedham** in Suffolk Co., In "New" Norfolk Co., in 1793, **Name changed in 1836 to Dover**

District of Palmer: Hampden Co., Settled in 1716, **See Palmer**

District of Shelburne: Franklin Co., Settled in 1756, **See Shelburne**

District of Stoughtonham: Settled in 1637 in Massachusetts Bay Colony, In "Old" Norfolk Co. in 1643, In Suffolk Co. in 1679 **See Stoughtonham & Sharon**

Dorchester: Suffolk Co., Settled and **Inc. as Dorchester in 1630**, In Suffolk Co. in 1630, In "New" Norfolk Co. in 1793, Annexed by Boston in 1870 and once again was in Suffolk Co.

Douglas: Worcester Co., Settlement in 1721 called New Sherburn, **Inc. in 1746 as Douglas**

Dover (1): "Old" Norfolk Co., Prev. to 1623 called Wecohamet, Settlements in 1623 called Cochecho and Hilton's Point, Called Bristol in 1633, Called Dover in 1637, Called Northem in 1639, Renamed Dover in 1639, **Inc. in 1643 as Dover MA in "Old" Norfolk Co., Inc. in 1679 as Dover NH**

Dover (2): Norfolk Co., Settlement in 1640 called Springfield Parish a V. in Dedham in "Old" Norfolk Co., **Inc. in 1784 as District of Dedham,** In "New" Norfolk Co. in 1793, **Name changed in 1836 to Dover**

Dracut: Middlesex Co., Prev. to 1653 called Augumtoocooke, Settled in 1653 as Dracut V., **Inc. in 1701 as Dracut**

Dudley: Worcester Co., Settled in 1714, **Inc. in 1732 as Dudley**

Dunstable: Middlesex Co., Settled in 1656 as part of Duxbury, Called Dunstable Township in 1661, **Inc. in 1673 as Dunstable**, The northern section of Dunstable became Dunstable **NH** in 1746, Dunstable **NH** name changed to Nashua **NH** in 1836

Duxborrow: Plymouth Co., **Alias of Duxbury**

Duxbury: Plymouth Co., Prev. to 1624 called Mattakeesett, Settlement in 1624 called Duxbury aka Duxborrow, **Inc. in 1637 as Duxbury**

East Andover: Essex Co., Settled in 1789, **See Andover ME**

East Andover P.: Essex Co., **See Andover ME**

East Bridgewater: Plymouth Co., Settled in 1630 as part of Plymouth, Part of Bridgewater in 1636, Part of Duxbury in 1637, **Inc. in 1823 as East Bridgewater**

East Chelmsford: Middlesex Co., Settled in 1633, **See Lowell**

East Enfield: Hampshire Co., Settled in 1706 as a V. in Springfield, **See Somers**

East Medway: Norfolk Co., Settled in 1657, **See Millis**

East Sudbury: Middlesex Co., Settled in 1638, Called Sudbury P. in 1639, **Inc. in 1780 as East Sudbury, Renamed Wayland in 1835**

Eastham: Barnstable Co., Settlement in 1644 called Nauset, **Inc. in 1651 as Eastham**

Easthampton: Hampshire Co., Settlement in 1664 called Pascommuck a V. in Northampton, Called Easthampton in 1785, **Inc. in 1809 as Easthampton**

Easton: Bristol Co., Settled in 1694 as part of Taunton, **Inc. in 1725 as Easton**

Edgartown: Dukes Co., Settlement in 1642 called Great Harbor in Dukes Co, **NY, Inc. in 1671 as Edgartown, Dukes Co., NY, Became Edgartown, Dukes Co., MA in 1691**

Elbows P.: Hampden Co., Settled in 1716, **See Palmer**

Enfield: Hampshire Co., Settled in 1679 by families from Salem, **Inc. in 1683 as Enfield, Ceded to CT in 1749**

Essex: Essex Co., Settled in 1634 as a V. in Ipswich, **Inc. in 1819 as Essex**

Exeter: Norfolk Co., Settled in 1638, **Inc. in 1639 as Exeter**, In "Old" Norfolk Co. in 1643, In Rockingham Co. **NH** in 1679

Fairhaven: Bristol Co., Settled in 1659 as a V. in Dartmouth, A V. in New Bedford in 1787, **Inc. in 1812 as Fairhaven**

Falls Flight: Franklin Co., **See Bernardston**

Falltown P.: Franklin Co., **See Bernardston**

Falmouth: Barnstable Co., "Discovered" and named Falmouth by Bartholomew Gosnold in 1602, Prev. to 1660 called Suckanesset, Settled in 1660 as Falmouth, **Inc. in 1686 as Falmouth**

Fitchburg: Worcester Co., Settled in 1730 as part of Lunenburg, **Inc. in 1764 as Fitchburg**

Florida: Berkshire Co., Settled in 1783 as part of Bernardston, **Inc. in 1805 as Florida**

Foxboro: Norfolk Co., **Alias of Foxborough,** Note: (While the official name is Foxborough, the P.O. Prefers the alias Foxboro and town signage has Foxboro.)

Foxborough: Norfolk Co., Settled in 1704 as Foxborough, **Inc in 1778 as Foxborough** aka Foxboro, In "New" Norfolk Co. when it was formed in 1793

Framingham: Middlesex Co., Settlement in 1647, Called Framlingham as in Framlingham in Suffolk England in 1660, **Inc. in 1700 as Framingham** following the death in 1699 of the founder Thomas Danforth

Framlingham: Middlesex Co., **See Framingham** (Note: Why the "L" was dropped from the name in 1700 is unknown.)

Freetown: Bristol Co., Settled in 1649 as part of Plymouth, **Inc. in 1683 as Freetown** in Plymouth Co., In Bristol Co. in 1793

Gageborough: Berkshire Co., Settlement in 1767 called Gageborough in honor of the British Gen. Thomas Gage, **Inc. in 1771 as Gageborough**, Not surprisingly, **reorganized and Inc. in 1778 with the name changed to Windsor**

Gay Head: Dukes Co., Settlement in 1662 called Gay Head aka Aquinnah, **Inc. in 1870 as Gay Head, Name changed to Aquinnah in 1997**

Georgeana: Gorges Patent, Settlement in 1624 called Agamenticus P., Called Bristol in 1636, **Inc. in 1642 as City of Georgeana** (1st city in America) by order of King Charles I, Claimed by MBC in 1652 as part of the newly formed York County with a portion of Georgeana Inc. as York **ME, See York ME**

Georgetown: Essex Co., Settlement in 1639 called New Rowley V. in Rowley, **Inc. in 1838 as Georgetown**

Gerry: Worcester Co., Settled in 1751, **Inc. in 1786 as Gerry, Name changed to Phillipston in 1814**

Gill: Franklin Co., Settled in 1776, **Inc. in 1793 as Gill**

Gloucester: Essex Co., Settlement in 1623 called Nantasket aka Cape Ann Colony established as a fishing village by the Dorchester Company, **Inc. in 1642 as Gloucester**

Grafton: Worcester Co., Prev. to 1647 called Hassanamessit a Praying Indian Village, Settlement in 1647 called Grafton, **Inc. in 1735 as Grafton**

Great Barrington: Berkshire Co., Settled in 1726, Called North Parish V. in Sheffield in 1742, **Inc. in 1761 as Great Barrington**

Great Harbor: Dukes Co., Settled in 1642, **See Edgartown**

Greenfield: Franklin Co., Settled in 1686 as part of Deerfield, **Inc. in 1753 as Greenfield**

Green's Harbour: Plymouth Co., Settled in 1632, **See Marshfield**

Groton: Middlesex Co., Prev. to 1655 called Petepawag P., Settled and **Inc. in 1655 as Groton**

Hadley: Hampshire Co., Settlement in 1659 called Hadley, **Inc. in 1661 as Hadley**, It was a large town in area that included territory that would later become the towns of Hatfield, Amherst, S. Hadley, Granby and Belchertown.

Halifax: Plymouth Co., Prev. to 1669 called Monponset, Settled in 1669 as part of Western Parish of Plymouth, Part of Plympton in 1707, **Inc. in 1734 as Halifax**

Hamilton: Essex Co., Settlement in 1638 called The Hamlet in Ipswich, **Inc. in 1793 as Hamilton**

Hampton: Norfolk Co., Settlement in 1638 called Hampton, **Inc. in 1639 as Hampton**, In "Old" Norfolk Co. in 1643, In Rockingham Co., **NH** in 1679, Note: (Along with Exeter, the 1st permanent `European settlements in what would become NH)

Hanover: Plymouth Co., Settled in 1649 as part of Scituate, **Inc. in 1727 as Hanover**

Hardwick: Worcester Co., Settlement in 1737 called Hardwick, **Inc. in 1739 as Hardwick**

Hartsville: Berkshire Co., A V. in New Marlborough

Harwich: Barnstable Co., Settled in 1670 as part of Yarmouth, **Inc. in 1694 as Harwich**

Hassanamessit: Worcester Co., A Praying Indian Village, **See Grafton**

Hatfield: Hampshire Co., Settlement in 1661 called Hatfield, **Inc. in 1670 as Hatfield**

Haverhill: Essex Co., Settlement in 1640 called Pentucket, **Inc. in 1641 as Haverhill.** In "Old" Norfolk Co. in 1643, In Essex Co. in 1679 after "Old" Norfolk Co. was abolished.

Heath: Franklin Co., Settlement in 1765 called Heath, **Inc. in 1785 as Heath**

Hingham: Plymouth Co., Settled in 1633 as part of Plymouth called Bare Cove, **Inc. in 1635 as Hingham** in Suffolk Co., In "New" Norfolk Co. in 1793, In Plymouth Co. in 1803

Holden: Worcester Co., Settled in 1673 as part of Worcester, **Inc. in 1741 as Holden**

Holliston: Middlesex Co., Settlement in 1659 called Awassamog (First Nipmuc Praying Indian Village), **Inc. in 1724 as Holliston**

Holmes Hole: Dukes Co., Settled in 1660 a Port V. in Tisbury, aka Vineyard Haven

Holyoke: Hampden Co., Settlement in 1745 called Third Parish Village of Springfield aka North Parish and Irish Parish, **Inc. in 1850 as Holyoke**

Hopedale: Worcester Co., Settled in 1660 as part of Mendon, Part of Milford in 1780, A V. in Milford in 1841, **Inc. in 1886 as Hopedale**

Hopkinton: Middlesex Co., Settled and **Inc. in 1715 as Hopkinton**, Formed from Common Lands and Moguncoy P.

Housatonic: Berkshire Co., Alias of Outhotonnock

Housatonic Township # 1: Berkshire Co., Settled in 1735, **See Tryingham**

Housatonic Township # 4: Berkshire Co., Settled in 1750, **See Sandisfield**

Hubbardstown: Worcester Co., Settled in 1737 as part of Rutland, **Inc. in 1767 as Hubbardstown**

Hudson: Middlesex Co., Settled in 1699 as part of Marlborough, **Inc. in 1866 as Hudson**

Hull: Plymouth Co., Settlement in 1622 called Nantasket in Plymouth Colony, **Inc. in 1644 as Hull** in Suffolk Co., In the "New" Norfolk Co. in 1793, Hull and Hingham opted to be in Plymouth Co. in 1803

Huntington: Hampshire Co., Settlement in 1769 called Norwich, **Inc. in 1773 as Norwich, Name changed in 1775 to Huntington**

Huntstown: Franklin Co., Settled in 1743, **See Ashfield**

Hutchinson: Worcester Co., Settlement in 1720 called Northwest District of Rutland, **Inc. in 1774 as Hutchinson, Renamed Barre in 1776**

Indian Town: Berkshire Co., Settlement in 1734 called Indian Town by founding English Missionaries for the benefit of the Mahican Tribe, Chartered in 1737 as Indian Town, **Inc. in 1739 as Stockbridge**, Note: (Sadly, the Mahican Tribe Indians that gave assistance to the colonists during the French and Indian Wars and later during the Revolutionary War were forced to relocate to New York State and then to Wisconsin.)

Ipswich: Essex Co., Settlement in 1630 called Agawam, **Inc. in 1634 as Ipswich**

Irish Parish: Hampden Co., **Alias of Third Parish Village of Springfield**

Jeffrey's Creek: Essex Co., Settled in 1629, **See Manchester**

Jeffries Creek: Essex Co., Settled in 1633 as a V. in Ipswich aka Jeffries Neck

Jeffries Neck: Essex Co., Alias of Jeffries Creek

Kingston: Plymouth Co., Prev. to 1620 called Wetcketuket, Settled in 1620 as the Northern part of Plymouth, **Inc. in 1726 as Kingston**

Lancaster: Worcester Co., Settlement in 1643 called Nashaway, 1653 **Inc. in 1653 as Lancaster on the Nashua, Name later changed to Lancaster**

Lancaster on the Nashua: Worcester Co., **See Lancaster**

Lawrence: Essex Co., Settled in 1655 as part of Methuen and Andover, **Inc. in 1847 as Lawrence**

Lee: Berkshire Co., Settled in 1760, **Inc. in 1777 as Lee**

Leicester: Worcester Co., Settled in 1713, **Inc. in 1714 as Leicester**

Lexington: Middlesex Co., Settled in 1642 as part of Cambridge, Called Cambridge Farms Parish in 1691, **Inc. in 1713 as Lexington**

Leyden: Franklin Co., Settled in 1737, **Inc. in 1809 as Leyden**

Lincoln: Middlesex Co., Settled in 1654 as part of Concord, **Inc. in 1754 as Lincoln**

Little Compton: Bristol Co., Settlement in 1675 called Sakonnet, **Inc. in 1682 as Little Compton in Plymouth Colony, Ceded to RI in 1747**

Littleton: Middlesex Co., Prev. to 1686 called by the Indian name of Nashoba P. a Praying Indian Village, Settled in 1686, **Inc. in 1715 as Littleton**

Longmeadow: Hampden Co., Settlement in 1644 called The Farmland in Springfield, **Inc. in 1786 as Longmeadow**

Lowell: Middlesex Co., Settled in 1633 as part of Chelmsford, Called East Chelmsford in 1655, **Inc. in 1826 as Lowell**

Ludlow: Hampden Co., Settlement in 1751 called Stoney Hill a V. in Springfield, **Inc. in 1774 as Ludlow**

Lunenburg: Worcester Co., Settled in 1718, **Inc. in 1728 as Lunenburg**

Lynn: Essex Co., Settlement in 1629 called Saugus (Nipmuck name), **Inc. in 1631 as Saugus, Name changed to Lynn in 1637**

Lynn Village: Essex Co., Settled in 1639, **See Reading**

Lynnfield: Essex Co., Part of Lynn **Inc. in 1782 as Lynnfield**

Malden: Middlesex Co., Settlement in 1640 in part of Charlestown V. called Mystic Side, **Inc. in 1649 as Malden**

Manamooskeagin: Plymouth Co., Settled in 1668, **See Abington**

Manchaug: Worcester Co., Settled in 1704, **See Sutton**

Manchester: Essex Co., **See Manchester-by-the-Sea**

Manchester-by-the-Sea: Essex Co., Settlement in 1629 called Jeffrey's Creek, **Inc. in 1645 as Manchester, About 1850 called Manchester-by-the-Sea** to avoid confusion with another railway station in Manchester NH, **Officially renamed Manchester-by-the-Sea in 1989**

Mansfield: Bristol Co., Settled in 1637 as part of Taunton, Part of Norton in 1710, **Inc. in 1775 as Mansfield**

Marble Harbor: Essex Co., Settled in1629 as part of Salem, **See Marblehead**

Marblehead: Essex Co., Seasonal fishing village in 1626 called Massebequash, Settlement in 1629 called Marble Harbor a part of Naumkeag, Part of Salem called Marble Harbor in 1630, Called Marblehead V. in Salem in 1633, **Inc. in 1649 as Marblehhead**

Maremount: Suffolk Co., Settled in 1625, **See Quincy**

Marlboro: Middlesex Co., **Alias of Marlborough**

Marlborough: Middlesex Co., Settlement in 1657 called Marlborough, **Inc. in 1660 as Marlborough** aka Marlboro

Marshfield: Plymouth Co., Settlement in 1629 called Marshfield V. in Plymouth Colony, **Inc. in 1640 as Marshfield**

Massebequash: Essex Co., A seasonal fishing V. in 1626, **See Marblehead**

Mattacheese: Plymouth Co., **See Yarmouth**

Mattakeesett: Plymouth Co., **See Duxbury**

Mattapoisett: Plymouth Co., Settlement in 1750 called Mattapoisett V. in Plymouth, **Inc. in 1857 as Mattapoisett**

Medfield: Norfolk Co., Settlement in 1649 called New Dedham a V. in Dedham in "Old" Norfolk Co., **Inc. in 1651 as Medfield** in "Old" Norfolk Co., In Suffolk Co in 1679, In "New" Norfolk Co. in 1793

Medford: Middlesex Co., Settled in 1630 in part of Charlestown V. called Mystic Side, **Inc. in 1684 as Medford**

Medway: Norfolk Co., Settlement in "Old" Norfolk Co. called Medway in 1657 by residents of Medfield, **Inc. in 1713 as Medway** in Suffolk Co., In "New" Norfolk Co. in 1793

Melrose: Middlesex Co., Settlement in 1629 called Pond Fielde, Part of Charlestown V. in 1633, **Inc. in 1850 as Melrose**

Mendon: Worcester Co., Settled (Unofficial) in 1640 by residents of Roxbury, Deed in 1662 from Nipmuck Chief Great John legitimized settlement, **Inc. in 1667 as Mendon** in Essex Co., In Suffolk Co. in 1671, In Worcester Co. in 1731

Menotomy: Middlesex Co., Settlement in 1635 called Menotomy a V. in Cambridge, A V. in West Cambridge in 1807, **Inc. in 1867 as Arlington**

Merrimac: Essex Co., Settled in 1638 as part of Merrimac P., Part of Salisbury in 1639, Called West Amesbury a V. in Amesbury in 1667, **Inc. in 1876 as Merrimac**

Merrimac P.: Essex Co., **See Amesbury & Merrimac**

Methuen: Essex Co., Settled in 1642 as part of Haverhill, **Inc. in 1725 as Methuen**

Middleborough: Plymouth Co., Settlement in 1661 called Nemasket and later called Middlebury, **Inc. in 1669 as Middleborough**

Middlebury: Plymouth Co., **See Middleborough**

Middleton: Essex Co., Settled in 1659 as parts of Salem, Andover, Boxford and Topsfield, **Inc. in 1728 as Middleton**

Milford: Worcester Co., Settlement in 1662 called Mill River a V. in Mendon, **Inc. in 1780 as Milford**

Mill River: Essex Co., Settled in 1662, **See Milford**

Mill River Village: Berkshire Co., A V. in New Marlborough

Millbury: Worcester Co., Settlement in 1716 called Second Parish in Sutton aka North Parish, **Inc. in 1813 as Millbury**

Millis: Norfolk Co., Settled in 1657 as part of Dedham, Called East Medway V. in Medway in 1713, **Inc. in 1885 as Millis**

Milton: Norfolk Co., Settled in 1640 as a V. in Dorchester in "Old" Norfolk Co., **Inc. in 1662 as Milton** in Suffolk Co., In the "New" Norfolk Co. in 1793

Mishawaum: Suffolk Co., Settled in 1624, **See Charlestown**

Mistick: Middlesex Co., Alias of Mystic Side, **See Medford & Malden**

Moguncoy P.: Middlesex Co., **See Hopkinton**

Monomuit: Barnstable Co., Settled in 1656, **See Chatham**

Monponset: Plymouth Co., Settled in 1669, **See Halifax**

Monson: Hampden Co., Settled in 1735 as a V. in Brimfield, **Inc. in 1775 as Monson**

Montague: Franklin Co., Settlement in 1715 called Peskeompskut, **Inc. in 1754 as Montague**

Monterey: Berkshire Co., Settled in 1735 as part of Housatonic Township, A V. in Housatonic Township in 1762, **Inc. in 1847 as Monterey**

Mount Wollaston: Suffolk Co., Settled in 1625, **See Quincy**

Muddy River Village: Norfolk Co., 1638 a V. in Boston, **See Brookline**

Musketaquid: Middlesex Co., **See Concord**

Mystic Side: Middlesex Co., Settled in 1630, **See Medford and Malden**

Nahant: Essex Co., Settled in 1630 as a part of Lynn, **Inc. in 1853 as Nahant**

Nantasket: Essex Co., Settled in 1622 as a V. in Plymouth Colony, **See Hull**

Nantucket: Nantucket Co., Settlement in 1641 called Nautucket aka Nautuckett, In Nautucket Co. NY in 1641, **Inc. in 1671 as Nantucket NY, Renamed Sharborn by NY in 1687, Transferred from NY to MA in 1691, Renamed Nantucket MA in 1795**

Nashaway: Worcester Co., Settled in 1643, **See Lancaster**

Nashoba: Middlesex Co., **See Littleton**

Natick: Middlesex Co., Settlement in 1651 called Natick a Praying Indian P., **Inc. in 1781 as Natick**

Naumkeag: Essex Co., Settled in 1626, **See Salem**

Nauset: Barnstable Co., Settled in 1644, **See Eastham**

Nautucket: Nantucket Co., Settled in 1641, aka Nautuckett, **See Nantucket**

Needham: Norfolk Co., Settled in 1680 as part of Dedham in Suffolk Co., **Inc. in 1711 as Needham** in Suffolk Co., In "New" Norfolk Co. when it was formed in 1793

Nemasket: Plymouth Co., Settled in 1661, **See Middleborough**

New Bedford: Bristol Co., Settled in 1652 as part of Dartmouth, New Bedford was a V. in Dartmouth in 1654, New Bedford V. along with Acushnet V. and Fairhaven V. seceded from Dartmouth and **Inc. in 1787 as New Bedford**, Fairhaven V. separated from New Bedford and Inc. in 1812 as Fairhaven, Acushnet V. separated from New Bedford and Inc. in 1860 as Acushnet

New Braintree: Worcester Co., Settled in 1709, **Inc. in 1751 as New Braintree**

New Dedham: Norfolk Co., Settled in 1649, **See Medfield**

New Ipswich-Canada: Worcester Co., Settled in 1755, **See Winchendon**

New Marlborough: Berkshire Co., Settled in 1738, **Inc. in 1759 as New Marlborough**

New Meadows: Essex Co., Settled in 1643, **See Topsfield**

New Plymouth: Plymouth Co., Settled in 1620, **See Plymouth**

New Rowley: Essex Co., Settled in 1639, **See Georgetown**

New Roxbury Village: Worcester Co., Settled in 1686, **See Woodstock CT**

New Sherburn: Worcester Co., Settled in 1721, **See Douglas**

Newbury: Essex Co., Settled in 1635 by Immigrants from Ipswich, **Inc. in 1635 as Newbury**

Newburyport: Essex Co., Settled in 1635 as part of Newbury., **Inc. in 1764 as Newburyport**

Newe Towne: Middlesex Co., Settled in 1630, **See Cambridge**

Newton: Middlesex Co., Settled in 1630 as part of Newe Towne V. in Cambridge, Part of Cambridge in 1636, **Inc. in 1688 as Cambridge Village, Renamed Newtown in 1691, Renamed Newton in 1766,** Note: (Without moving, one could have been born in Cambridge, married in Cambridge Village, have children in Newtown and die In Newton.)

Newtown: Middlesex Co., Settled in 1630, **See Newton**

Newtown Village: Essex: Settled in 1643 as a V. in Salisbury, **See Salisbury & Amesbury**

Nonotuck: Hampshire Co., **Alias of Norwottuck**

Norfolk: Norfolk Co., Settled in 1660 as part of Boston in Suffolk Co., Abandoned in 1676 due to King Philip's War, Resettled in 1795 in "New" Norfolk Co., **Inc. in 1870 as Norfork**

North Andover: Essex Co., Settled in 1641 as part of Andover, A V. in Andover in 1709, **Inc. in 1855 as North Andover**

North Brookfield: Worcester Co., Settled in 1664, **Inc. in 1812 as North Brookfield**

North Parish (1): Berkshire Co., A V. in Sheffield

North Parish (2): Hampden Co., Alias of Third Parish Village of Springfield, **See Holyoke**

North Parish (3): Worcester Co., Alias of Second Parish in Millbury, **See Millbury**

North Reading: Middlesex Co., Settled in 1651 as part of Reading, **Inc. in 1853 as North Reading**

North Taunton: Bristol Co., Settled in 1639 as part of Taunton, **See Norton**

North Westport: Bristol Co., Settled in 1670 as a V. in Westport

Northborough: Worcester Co., Settled in 1660 as part of Marlborough, **Inc. in 1775 as Northborough**

Northampton: Hampshire Co., Prev. to 1654 called Norwottuck aka Nonotuck, Settled in 1654 as Horthampton, **Inc. in 1654 as Northampton**

Northbridge: Worcester Co., Settled in 1704 as part of Mendon, Part of Uxbridge in 1727, **Inc. in 1772 as Northbridge**

Northfield: Franklin Co., Settlement in 1673 called Squawkeag, Called Northfield in 1714, **Inc. in 1723 as Northfield, Inc. in 1764 as Hinsdale VT.**

Northwest District of Rutland: Worcester Co., Settled in 1720, **See Barre**

Norton: Bristol Co., Settled in 1639 as part of Taunton, Called North Taunton V. in Taunton in 1669, **Inc. in 1710 as Norton** (Contraction of North Taunton)

Norwich: Hampshire Co., Settlement in1769 called Norwich, **Inc. in 1776 as Norwich, Renamed Huntington in 1775**

Norwottuck: Hampshire Co., Settlement in 1654 called Norwottuck aka Nonotuck, **See Northampton**

Oak Bluffs: Dukes Co., Settled in 1642 as part of Edgartown (Dukes Co., **NY**), Part of Edgartown (Dukes Co., **MA**) in 1691, **Inc. in 1880 as Oak Bluffs**

Orleans: Barnstable Co., Settled in 1693 as part of Eastham, **Inc. in 1797 as Orleans,** Note: (Orleans was named in honor of Orleans, France recognizing France's support for the 13 colonies during the Revolution and, as they had been captured twice by the British during the war., they did not want an English name.)

Outhotonnock: Berkshire Co., Settlement in 1725 called Outhotonnock aka Housatonic, **See Sheffield**

Oxford: Worcester Co., Settlement in 1686 called Oxford by Huguenots (French Protestants), **Inc. in 1713 as Oxford**

Palmer: Hampden Co., Settlement in 1716 called Elbows P., Called District of Palmer in 1752, **Inc. in 1775 as Palmer** in Hampshire Co., In Hampden Co. in 1812

Parsons: Essex Co., Settled in 1635 as part of Newbury, **Inc. in Feb 1819 as Parsons, Name changed in Jun 1820 to West Newbury**

Pascommuck: Hampshire Co., Settled in 1664, **See Easthampton**

Pawtucket: Bristol Co., Settled in 1671 as a V. in Rehoboth, **Merged in 1860 with West Pawtucket and transferred to RI, See Pawtucket RI**

Paxton: Worcester Co., Settled in 1749 as part of Leicester and Rutland, **Inc. in 1765 as Paxton**

Peabody: Essex Co., Settled in 1754 as part of Danvers V. in Salem, Part of town of Danvers in 1757, **Inc. in 1855 as Peabody**

Pelham: Hampshire Co., Settlement in 1738 called Pelham, **Inc. in 1743 as Pelham**

Pembroke: Plymouth Co., Settled in 1650 as part of Duxbury, **Inc. in 1712 as Pembroke**

Pentucket: Essex Co., Settlement in 1640 called Pentucket, **See Haverhill**

Pepperell: Middlesex Co., Settled in 1720 as part of Groton, **Inc. in 1753 as Pepperell**

Pequoiag: Worcester Co., **See Athol**

Peskeompskut: Franklin Co., Settled in 1715, **See Montague**

Petepawag P.: Middlesex Co., **See Groton**

Petersham: Worcester Co., Settlement in 1733 called Petersham (Pronounced "Peters-ham"), **Inc. in 1754 as Petersham**

Phillipston: Worcester Co., Settlement in 1751 called Phillipston, **Inc. in 1786 as Gerry, Name changed to Phillipston in 1814**

Pittsfield: Berkshire Co., Settlement in 1750 called Pontoosuck, **Inc. in 1753 as Pittsfield P., Name changed to Pittsfield in 1761**

Pittsfield P.: Berkshire Co., Settlement in 1750 called Pontoosuck, **Inc. in 1753 as Pittsfield P., Name changed to Pittsfield in 1761**

Plantation of Dorchester-Canada: Worcester Co., Settlement in 1736 called Plantation of Dorchester-Canada , **See Ashburnham**

Plymouth: Plymouth Co., Settlement in 1620 called New Plymouth aka Plymouth

Plympton: Plymouth Co., Prev. to 1660 called Wenatukset, Settled in 1660 as part of Plymouth, Called Western Parish in Plymouth in 1662, **Inc. in 1707 as Plympton**

Pompositticut P.: Middlesex Co., Settlement in 1660 called Pompositticut, **See Stow**

Pond Fielde: Middlesex Co., Settlement in 1629 called Pond Fielde, **See Melrose**

Pontoosuck: Berkshire Co., Settlement in 1750 called Pontoosuck, **See Pittsfield**

Princeton: Worcester Co., Settled in 1743 as part of Rutland, **Inc. in 1771 as Princeton**

Provincetown: Barnstable Co., Seasonal fishing village in 1665, Settlement in 1700 called

Provincetown, **Inc. in 1727 as Provincetown,** Note: (Where the *Mayflower* was first anchored and where a few passengers first went ashore.)

Pullen Poynt: Suffolk Co., A grazing area for Winnisimmet residents called Pullen Poynt in 1630, Pullen Poynt annexed by Boston in 1632, Settlement in 1637 called Pullen Poynt V. in Boston, **See Chelsea**

Quaboag P.: Worcester Co., Settlement in 1660 called Quaboag P., **See Brookfield**

Quincy: Norfolk Co., Settlement in 1625 called Mount Wollaston, Called Maremount in 1626, A part of Dorchester in 1630, Annexed by Boston in 1634, A V. in Braintree in 1640, In "Old Norfolk Co. in 1643, In Suffolk Co. in 1679, **Inc. in 1792 as** Quincy in Suffolk Co., In the "New" Norfolk Co. in 1793, **Inc. as the City of Quincy in 1888**

Quinsigamond: Worcester Co., Settlement in 1673 called Quinsigamond, Burned and abandoned in King Philip's War in 1675, Resettled about 1680, **Inc. in 1684 as Quinsigamond, Renamed Worcester shortly after Inc. in 1684**

Raynham: Bristol Co., Settled in 1639 as part of Taunton, **Inc. in 1731 as Raynham**

Reading: Middlesex Co., Settled in 1638 as part of Lynn called Lynn Village, **Ten sq. miles split off from Lynn in 1644 and Inc. as Reading**

Rehoboth: Bristol Co.; Settlement in 1643 called Rehoboth; **Inc. in 1645 as Rehoboth** which included territory that would become Seekonk & East Pawtucket **RI**; parts of Attleboro, North Attleboro, Swansea & Somerset **MA,** along with Barrington, Bristol, Warren, Pawtucket, Cumberland and Woonsocket **RI**

Revere: Suffolk Co., Settled in 1630 as part of Boston, **Inc. in 1871 as Revere** named in honor of Paul Revere

Richmond: Berkshire Co., Settled in 1760 as part of Stockbridge, **Inc. in 1765 as Richmond**

Rochester: Plymouth Co., Settlement in 1679 called Sippican, **Inc. in 1686 as Rochester**

Rockland: Plymouth Co., Settled in 1673 as part of Manamooskeagin (Land of many beavers), Part of Abington V. in 1706, Part of Abington in 1712, **Inc. in 1874 as Rockland**

Rockport: Essex Co., Settled in 1623 as part of Cape Ann, Part of Gloucester in 1642, **Inc. in 1840 as Rockport**

Rocksberry: Suffolk Co., Settled in 1630, **See Roxbury**

Rocky Nook: Plymouth Co., Settlement in 1623 called Rocky Nook a V. in Plymouth, A V. in Kingston in 1726

Rowley: Essex Co., Settlement in 1638 by passengers arriving on the *John of London*, **Inc. in 1639 as Rowley**

Rowley Village: Essex Co., Settled in 1646 as a V. in Rowley, A V. in Boxford in 1685

Roxbury: Suffolk Co., Settlement in 1630 called Rocksberry a V. in Boston, **Inc. in 1846 as Roxbury**

Rumney Marsh: Suffolk Co., Settlement in 1630 called Rumney March, Annexed by Boston in 1634, **See Chelsea**

Rutland: Worcester Co., Settled in 1686, **Inc. in 1713 as Rutland**

Sagamore: Barnstable Co., Settled in 1640 as a V. in Sandwich, A V. in Bourne in 1884

Sakonnet: Bristol Co. Settlement in 1675 called Sakonnet, **See Little Compton**

Salem: Essex Co., Settlement in 1626 called Naumkeag, **Inc. in 1629 as Salem**

Salem Village: Essex Co., Settlement in 1626 called Salem Village, Called Salem Village a V. in Salem in 1629, Called Danvers a V. in Salem in 1752, **Inc. in 1757 as Danvers**

Salisbury: Essex Co., Settlement in 1637 by John Bailey, Called Merrimac P. in 1638, **Inc. in Sep 1639 as Colchester, Name changed in Oct 1639 to Salisbury.** In "Old" Norfolk Co. in 1643, In Essex Co. in 1679 when "Old" Norfolk Co. was abolished

Sandisfield: Berkshire Co., Settlement in 1750 called Housatonic Township # 4, **Inc. in 1762 as Sandisfield**

Sandwich: Barnstable Co., Settlement in 1637 called Sandwich a V. in Plymouth, **Inc. in 1639 as**

Sandwich

Saugus (1): Essex Co., Settlement in 1629 called Saugus V., **Inc. in 1631 as Saugus, Name changed to Lynn in 1637**

Saugus (2): Essex Co., Settlement in 1629 as part of Saugus V., Split from Lynn and **Inc. in 1815 as Saugus**

Scituate: Plymouth Co., Settled in 1627 as part of Plymouth, **Inc. in 1636 as Scituate**

Second Parish of Lancaster: Worcester Co., Settlement in 1720 called Second Parish of Lancaster aka Crocksett, **See Sterling**

Second Parish of Sutton: Worcester Co., **See Millbury**

Second Precinct of Stoughton: Suffolk Co., **See Stoughtonham & Sharon**

Seekonk: Bristol Co., Settled in 1636 as part of Rehoboth, **Inc. in 1812 as Seekonk**

Sharon: Norfolk Co., Settled in 1637 as part of Massachusetts Bay Colony, In "Old" Norfolk Co. in 1643, Called Second Precinct of Stoughton in 1740 in Suffolk Co., Called District of Stoughtonham in 1765 in Stoughton in Suffolk Co., **Inc. in 1775 as Stoughtonham** in Suffolk Co., **Renamed Sharon in 1783** in Suffolk Co. In "New" Norfolk Co. in 1793

Shawshin: Middlesex Co., Settlement in 1652 called Shawshin, **See Billerica**

Sheffield: Berkshire Co., Settlement in 1725 called Outhotonnock aka Housatonic, **Inc. in 1733 as Sheffield**

Shelburne: Franklin Co., Settlement in 1756 called Deerfield Northwest a V. in Deerfield, **Inc. in 1775 as Shelburne**

Sherborn: Middlesex Co., Settlement in 1652 called Boggestow, **Inc. in 1674 as Sherburne and later renamed Sherborn**

Sherburne: Middlesex Co. Settlement in 1652 called Boggestow, **Inc. in 1674 as Sherburne,** See Sherborn

Shirley: Middlesex Co., Settled in 1720 as part of Groton, **Inc. in 1753 as Shirley**

Shrewsbury: Worcester Co., Settlement in 1720 called Shrewsbury, **Inc. in 1727 as Shrewsbury**

Sippican: Plymouth Co., Settlement in 1679 called Sippican, **See Rochester**

Somers: Hampshire Co., Settlement in 1706 called East Enfield in Springfield, **Inc. in 1734 as Somers, Ceded in 1749 to CT**

Somerville: Middlesex Co., Settlement in 1629 called Charlestown Beyond the Neck, **Inc. in 1842 as Somerville**

South Andover: Essex Co., Settlement in 1641 as South Andover a V. in Andover

South Parish of Worcester: Settlement in 1714 called South Parish of Worcester, **See Ward and Auburn**

South Reading: Middlesex Co., Settlement in 1638 called Lynn Village in Lynn, Called South Reading V. in Reading in 1644, Split from Reading and **Inc. in 1812 as South Reading, Renamed Wakefield in 1812**

Southampton: Hampshire Co., Settled in 1654 as part of Northampton, **Inc. in 1775 as Southampton**

Southborough: Worcester Co., Settled in 1660 as part of Marlborough, **Inc. in 1727 as Southborough**

Southbridge: Worcester Co., Settled in 1730, **Inc. in 1816 as Southbridge**

Souther Towne: Bristol Co., Settled in 1649, Called Souther Towne ake Southerton in 1658, **See Stonington MA and Stonington CT**

Southerton: Bristol Co. **Alias of Souther Towne**

Southfield (1): Berkshire Co., A V. in New Marlborough

Southfield (2): Hampden Co., Settlement in 1674 called Southfield, **See Suffield**

Sowams: Bristol Co., Settlement in 1653 called Sowams, **Inc. in 1668 as Sowams, See Warren RI**

Spencer: Worcester Co., Settled in 1721 as part of Leicester, **Inc. in 1753 as Spencer**

Springfield: Hampden Co., Settlement in 1636 called Agawam P., **Inc. in 1641 as Springfield**

Springfield Parish: Norfolk Co., Settlement in 1640 called Springfield Parish a V. in Dedham, **See Dover**

Squawkeag: Franklin Co., Settlement in 1673 called Squawkeag, **See Northfield**

Sterling: Worcester Co., Settlement in 1720 called Second Parish of Lancaster aka Crocksett, **Inc. in 1781 as Sterling**

Stockbridge: Berkshire Co., Settlement in 1734 called Indian Town settled by missionaries for the Natives, Chartered in 1737 as Indian Town, **Inc. in 1739 as Stockbridge**

Stoneham: Middlesex Co., Settled in 1645 as part of Charlestown V., **Inc. in 1725 as Stoneham**

Stoney Hill: Hampden Co., Settlement in 1751 called Stoney Hill a V. in Springfield, **See Ludlow**

Stonington: Bristol Co., Settled in 1649, Called Souther Towne aka Southerton in 1658, In **CT** in 1662, **See Stonington CT**

Stoughton: Suffolk Co., Settlement in 1713 called Stoughton, In 1726 Stoughton became the nickname for the incorporated "Town of Stoughton"

Stoughton (Town of): Norfolk Co., Settlement in 1713 called Stoughton in the southwest part of Dorchester in Suffolk Co., **Inc in 1726 as. "Town of Stoughton"** in Suffolk Co., In the "new" Norfolk Co. when it was formed in 1793

Stoughtonham: Suffolk Co., Settled in 1637 in "Old" Norfolk Co., Called Second Precinct of Stoughton in 1740 in Stoughton in Suffolk Co., Called District of Stoughtonham in 1765 in Stoughton in Suffolk Co., **Inc. in 1775 as Stoughtonham** in Suffolk Co., **Renamed Sharon in 1783** in Suffolk Co.

Stow: Middlesex Co., Settlement in 1660 called Pompositticut P., Called Stow in 1681, **Inc. in 1683 as Stow**

Strawberry Banke: Norfolk Co., Settled in 1623, Called Strawberry Bank a V. in Massachusetts Bay Colony in 1630, Called Strawberry Banke a V. in the newly-formed "Old" Norfolk Co. in 1643, Became a V. in Portsmouth **NH** in 1679 when "Old" Norfolk Co. was abolished, Became a 10-acre history museum in Portsmouth **NH** in 1951

Sturbridge: Worcester Co., Settlement in 1729 called Sturbridge, **Inc. in 1738 as Sturbridge**

Sudbury: Middlesex Co., Settlement in 1638 Called Sudbury P., **Inc. in 1639 as Sudbury**

Sudbury P.: Middlesex Co., **See Sudbury**

Suffield: Hampden Co., Settlement in 1674 called Southfield, **Inc. in 1682 as Suffield MA**, Transferred to **CT** (Hartford Co.) in 1749

Sutton: Worcester Co., Settlement in 1704 called Manchaug, **Inc. in 1714 as Sutton**

Swampscott: Essex Co., Settled in 1629 as part of Lynn, **Inc. in 1852 as Swampscott**

Swansea: Bristol Co., Settled in 1662 as part of Rehoboth, **Inc. in 1667 as Swansea**

Taunton: Bristol Co., Settlement in 1636 called Cohannett, **Inc. in 1639 as Taunton**

Templeton: Worcester Co., Settlement in 1751 called Templeton, **Inc. in 1762 as Templeton**

Tewksbury: Middlesex Co., Settled in 1660 as part of Billerica, **Inc. in 1734 as Tewksbury**

The Farmland: Hampden Co., **See Longmeadow**

The Hamlet: Essex Co., **See Hamilton & Ipswich**

Third Parish Village of Springfield: Hampden Co., Settled in 1745 as a V. in Holyoke

Tisbury: Dukes Co., Settlement in 1660 called Tisbury in **Dukes Co. NY, Inc. in 1671 as Tisbury in Dukes Co. NY,** In Dukes Co. **MA** in 1691

Tiverton: Bristol Co., Settlement in 1629 called Tiverton, **Inc. in 1694 as Tiverton, Ceded in 1747 to RI** (Newport Co.)

Topsfield: Essex Co., Settlement in 1643 called New Meadows, Called Topsfield in 1648, **Inc. in 1650 as Topsfield**

Town of Stoughton: Norfolk Co., **See Stoughton (Town of)**

Townsend: Middlesex Co., **Alias of Townshend**

Townshend: Middlesex Co., Settlement in 1676 called Townshend, **Inc. in 1732 as Townshend,**

About 1780 aka Townsend which is now almost exclusively used, Note: (I would surmise that the descendants of Charles Viscount Townshend (1674-1738) who, while England's Secretary of State and member of the House of Lords, was an anti-Tory supporter of the American Revolution and the source of the name of Townshend.)

Trimountaine: Suffolk Co., **See Boston**

Truro: Barnstable Co., Settled in 1696 as part of Eastham, Called Truro in 1700, **Inc. in 1709 as Truro**

Turners Falls: Franklin Co., Settled in 1715 as a V. in Montague

Tyringham: Berkshire Co., Settlement in 1735 called Housatonic Township # 1, **Inc. in 1762 as Tyringham**

Unionville: Middlesex Co., Settled in 1750, **See Ashland**

Upper Ashuelot: Essex Co., Settlement in 1736 called Upper Ashuelot on the Ashuelot R. **See Keene NH**

Upton: Worcester Co., Settlement in 1728 called Upton, **Inc. in 1735 as Upton**

Uxbridge: Worcester Co., Settled in 1662 as part of Mendon, **Inc. in 1727 as Uxbridge**

Vineyard Haven: Dukes Co., Settled in 1660 as a port village in Tisbury, **aka Holmes Hole**

Wakefield: Middlesex Co., Settlement in 1638 called Lynn Village in Lynn, Called South Reading V. in Reading in 1644, Split from Reading and **Inc. in 1812 as South Reading, Renamed Wakefield in 1812**

Waltham: Middlesex Co., Settled in 1634 as a part of Watertown, **Inc. in 1738 as Waltham**

Wankinquag: Plymouth Co., Prev. to 1660 called Wankinquag, Settled in 1660 as a part of Plympton, **See Carver**

Wannamoisett: Bristol Co., Settled in 1643 as a V. in Rehoboth

Ward: Worcester Co., Settlement in 1714 called South Parish of Worcester, **Inc. in 1778 as Ward, 1837 name changed in 1837 to Auburn,** Note: (P.O. Complained that Ward was too similar to Ware.)

Ware: Hampshire Co., Settlement in 1717 called Ware, **Inc. in 1775 as Ware**

Wareham: Plymouth Co., Prev. to 1678 part of Agawam called Weweantic, Settled in 1678 as parts of Plymouth & Rochester, **Inc. in 1739 as Wareham**

Warren: Worcester Co., Settled in 1664 as part of Quaboag P., Part of Brookfield in 1718, **Inc. in 1741 as Western, Name changed to Warren in 1834**

Waterfield: Middlesex Co., Settlement in 1640 called Waterfield, **See Winchester**

Watertown: Middlesex Co., Settlement in 1630 called Watertown, **Inc. in 1630 as Watertown**

Watertown Falls: Middlesex Co., Settlement in 1642 as West Precinct of Watertown, **See Weston**

Wayland: Middlesex Co., Settled in 1639 as part of Sudbury P., **Inc. in 1780 as East Sudbury, Name changed in 1835 to Wayland**

Wellfleet: Barnstable Co., Prev. to 1651 called Billingsgate, Settled in 1651 as part of Eastham, **Inc. in 1763 as Wellfleet**

Wenatukset: Plymouth Co., Prev. to 1660 called Wenatukset, Settlement in 1660 called Plympton, **See Plympton**

Wenham: Essex Co., Settled in 1635 as part of Salem, **Inc. in 1643 as Wenham**

Wessagusset: Plymouth Co., Settlement in Aug 1622 called Wessagusset, **See Weymouth**

West Bridgewater: Plymouth Co., Settled in 1651 as part of Duxbury, Part of Bridgewater in 1656, **Inc. in 1822 as West Bridgewater**

West Cambridge: Middlesex Co., **See Menotomy and Arlington**

West Newbury: Essex Co., Settled in 1635 as part of Newbury, **Inc. in 1819 as Parsons, Name changed in 1820 to West Newbury**

West Pawtucket: Bristol Co., **See Pawtucket**

West Precinct of Watertown: Middlesex Co., Settlement in 1642 as West Precinct of Watertown aka

Watertown Falls, **See Weston**

West Springfield: Hampden Co., Settled in 1635 as part of Springfield, **Inc. in 1774 as West Springfield**

West Tisbury: Dukes Co., Settled in 1669 as part of Tisbury, Part of Tisbury **NY** in 1671, Part of Tisbury **MA** in 1691, **Inc. in 1892 as West Tisbury**

Westborough: Worcester Co., Settled in 1660 as part of Marlborough, **Inc. in 1717 as Westborough**

Western: Worcester Co., Settled in 1664 as part of Quaboag P., Part of Brookfield in 1718, **Inc. in 1741 as Western, Name changed to Warren in 1834**

Western Parish: Plymouth Co., **See Plympton**

Westfield: Hampden Co., Settlement in 1639 called Woronoco Village, Called Westfield Village in 1647, **Inc. in 1669 as Westfield**

Westfield Village: Hampden Co., **See Westfield**

Westford: Middlesex Co., Settled in 1635 as part of Chelmsford, **Inc. in 1729 as Westford**

Westham: Middlesex Co., Settlement in 1713 called Westham, **See Bellingham**

Westhampton: Hampshire Co., Settled in 1654 as part of Northampton, **Inc. in 1778 as Westhampton**

Westminster: Worcester Co., Settlement in 1737 called Westminster, **Inc. in 1770 as Westminster**

Weston: Middlesex Co., Settlement in 1642 called West Precinct of Watertown aka Watertown Falls, **Inc. in 1713 as Weston**

Westport: Bristol Co., Settled in 1670 as a V. in Dartmouth, Seceded from Dartmouth and **Inc. in 1787 as Westport**

Wetcketuket: Plymouth Co., **See Kingston**

Weweantic: Plymouth Co., **See Wareham**

Weymouth: Norfolk Co., Settlement in Aug 1622 called Wessagusset by settlers of the ill-fated Wessagusset Colony aka Weston Colony, Dissolved Mar 1623, Resettlement in Sep 1623 called Weymouth, **Inc. in 1630 as Wessagusset** in Suffolk Co., **Name changed to Weymouth in 1635,** In "Old" Norfolk Co. in 1643, In "New" Norfolk Co in 1793

Whately: Franklin Co., Settled in 1672 as part of Hatfield, **Inc. in 1771 as Whately**

Williamsburg: Hampshire Co., Settlement in 1735 called Williamsburg, **Inc. in 1775 as Williamsburg**

Wilmington: Middlesex Co., Settled in 1665 as parts of Woburn and Reading, **Inc. in 1730 as Wilmington**

Winchendon: Worcester Co., Settlement in 1753 called New Ipswich Canada, **Inc. in 1764 as Winchendon**

Winchester: Middlesex Co., Settlement in 1640 called Waterfield, Known in the 1700's as Black Horse Village, **Inc. in 1850 as Winchester**

Windsor: Berkshire Co., Settlement in 1767 called Gageborough in honor of the British Gen. Thomas Gage, **Inc. in 1771 as Gageborough, Reorganized and Inc. in 1778 with the name changed to Windsor**

Winnisimmet: Suffolk Co., Settlement in 1624 called Winnisimmet, **See Chelsea**

Woburn: Middlesex Co., Settlement in 1640 called Charlestowne Village, **Inc. in 1642 as Woburn**

Woodstock: Worcester Co., Settlement in 1686 called New Roxbury, Called Woodstock in 1690, **See Woodstock CT**

Worcester: Worcester Co., Settlement in 1673 called Quinsigamond, **Inc. in 1684 as Quinsigamond and renamed Worcester later in 1684**

Woronoco Village: Hampden Co., **See Westfield**

Worthington: Hampshire Co., Settlement in 1762 called Worthington, **Inc. in 1768 as Worthington**

Wrentham: Norfolk Co., Settled in 1660, **Inc. in 1673 as Wrentham** in "Old" Norfolk Co., Destroyed and abandoned in 1675 during King Philip's War, Resettled in 1677 in "Old" Norfolk

Co., In Suffolk Co. in 1679, In "New" Norfolk Co. in 1793
Yarmouth: Barnstable Co., Prev. to 1639 called Mattachesse, Settlement in 1639 called Yarmouth, **Inc. in 1639 as Yarmouth**

CHAPTER IV
NEW HAMPSHIRE

New Hampshire's State motto of "Live Free Or Die" was part of a toast from the Revolutionary War hero Gen. John Stark to his comrades-in-arms on 31 Jul 1809. He wrote, "Live Free Or Die, Death Is Not The Worst Of Evils"

Colonial Era Events in New Hampshire

1622: **Land Grant;** King James I granted the territory between the Salem and Merrimack Rivers to John Mason and Sir Ferdinando Gorges

1623: **Seasonal Fishing Villages Established;** Seasonal fishing villages had long been established at Odiorne Point, soon to be called Hilton's Point; Cochecho, later called Dover then Rye and six miles off the coast on the nine-island archipelago called the Isles of Shoals, later parts of Portsmouth NH (four islands) & Kittery ME (five islands)

1624: **First Permanent European Settlement;** The brothers Edward and William Hilton establish their homes and commence a fishery operation at the soon-to-be-named Hilton's Point, later part of Dover.

1629: **"New Hampshire";** John Mason receives a Royal Grant for that portion of the Province of Maine lying between the Merrimack and Piscataqua Rivers and names his grant New Hampshire

1638: **First "New Hampshire" Towns Settled;** Exeter was settled and inc. in 1638 by the exiled Rev. John Wheelwright and his followers. Hampton was settled in 1638 and inc. in 1639 by the notorious "scoundrel" Rev. Stephen Batchelder (Bachiler) and his followers

1641: **"Province of New Hampshire";** Massachusetts Bay Colony, citing grant ambiguities assumed political and legal control of the territory calling it their "Province of New Hampshire".

1679: **"New Hampshire Colony" Established by Royal Decree;** This newly-formed Colony also gains additional territory as **MA** abolished and ceded most of their Norfolk County to the new Colony. **MA** did retain some of Norfolk County on the north bank of the Merrimack River (Salisbury and Haverhill) with those towns being absorbed into Essex County.

1686: **Dominion of New England;** All of the America Colonies from the Delaware River to Penobscot

Bay in Maine were declared one entity, Dominion of New England, by King James II. From the outset, there was mass resistance to that concept because the colonists resented being stripped of rights by anyone, let alone a King who had strong ties to the Catholic Church.

1689: **Dominion of New England Collapses;** After King James II was overthrown in December 1688, the Colonies ousted Dominion officials and reverted to their previous structures and authorities.

1691: **"New Hampshire English Royal Colony";** William and Mary, joint monarchs of England and Scotland decreed that the New Hampshire Colony would be a self-ruled English Royal Colony.

1749: **New Hampshire Grants;** Between 1749 and 1764 Gov. Benning Wentworth of the New Hampshire Colony sold 135 land grants between the Connecticut River and Lake Champlain north of Massachusetts. This territory was rightfully claimed by New York, and while New York had done little to settle this territory, they disputed Wentworth's actions and told the newly granted towns that they would have to buy the same land again from New York.

1776: **New Hampshire Break away from England;** In January, 1776; New Hampshire was the first New England Colony to break all ties to England and on 04 Jul 1776 becomes one of the 13 Colonies to form the Union.

1788: **New Hampshire Statehood;** On 21 Jun 1788, New Hampshire became the 9th of the 13 original States to ratify the Constitution.

NEW HAMPSHIRE SETTLEMENTS

Populated Place

Amherst: Hillsborough Co., Settlement in 1733 called Narragansett No.3, Later called Souhegan No. 3, **Inc. in 1760 as Amherst**

Andover: Merrimack Co., Settlement in1761 called Emerisstown, 1746 called New Breton, 1779 Inc. in 1779 as Andover

Appledore: MBC, Settlement began in 1623 of the 9 habitable islands called Isles of Shoals, All 9 were **Inc. in 1661 as Appledore** by Massachusetts Bay Colony, Eventually 4 would be in **NH**: (Star, Lunging, Seavey and White), The other 5 (Appledore, Cedar, Duck, Malaga & Smuttynose) would be in **ME, See Isles of Shoals & Gosport**

Atkinson: Rockingham Co., Settled in 1728 as the western part of Plaistow, **Inc. in 1767 as Atkinson**

Barbadoes: Strafford Co., Settled in 1699 as a V. in Dover, **See Madbury**

Barrington: Strafford Co., Settlement in 1699 called Barrington, **Inc. in 1722 as Barrington**

Bloody Point: Rockingham Co., Settled in 1640 as a V. in Dover, **See Newington**

Bradford: Merrimack Co., Settlement in 1771 called New Bradford, Soon after called Bradfordton, **Inc. in 1787 as Bradford**

Bradfordton: Merrimack Co., **See Bradford**

Bridgewater: Grafton Co., **Inc. in 1788 as Bridgewater**

Bristol (1): Strafford Co., **See Dover**

Bristol (2): Grafton Co., Part of New Chester in 1753, Part of Bridgewater in 1788, **Inc. in 1819 as**

Bristol

Emerisstown: Merrimack Co., Settlement in 1761, **See Andover**

Chatham: Carroll Co., **Inc. in 1767 as Chatham**, Grantees did not settle until 1770 due to Indian hostilities

Chester: Rockingham Co., **Inc. in 1722 as Chester**

Chiswick: Grafton Co., Settled in 1763, **See Lisbon**

Cochecho P.: Stafford Co., Settled in 1623, **See Dover**

Colebrook: Coos Co., Original grant in 1762 in the name of Dryden not settled, Settlement in 1770 called Colebrook Town, **Inc. in 1796 as Colebrook**

Colebrook Town: Coos Co., Settled in 1770, **See Colebrook**

Concord (1): Grafton Co., Settled in 1763, **See Lisbon**

Concord (2): Merrimack Co., Settlement in 1725 called Penacook, **Inc. in 1734 as Rumford, Name changed in 1765 to Concord**

Cornish: Sullivan Co., Settlement in 1763 called Cornish, **Inc.in 1765 as Cornish**

Cornish Flat: Sullivan Co., **A V. in Cornish**

Croydon: Sullivan Co., **Inc. in 1763 as Croydon**

Deerfield: Rockingham Co., Prev. to 1766 a V. in Nottingham, **Inc. in 1766 as Deerfield**

Derryfield: Hillsborough Co., Settlement in 1722 called Old Harry's Town, Inc. in 1727 as Tyngstown in **MA** (ruled invalid), Inc. in 1751 as Derryfield, Renamed Manchester in 1846

Dover: Strafford Co., Prev. to 1623 called Wecohamet (Abenaki for "Pleasant Pines"), Called Cochecho P. in 1623, Settlement in 1624 by Edward and William Hilton called Hilton's Point, Called Bristol in 1633, Called Dover in 1637, Called Northem in 1639, Called Dover again in 1640, **Inc. in 1643 as Dover MA in "Old" Norfolk Co., Inc. in 1679 as Dover NH** in the newly established New Hampshire Colony, **Inc. in 1855 as the City of Dover**, Note: (First permanent European settlement in NH)

Dryden: Coos Co., **See Colebrook**

Dublin: Cheshire Co., Settlement in 1760 called Monadnock No. 3 aka North Monadnock, **Inc. in 1771 as Dublin**

Dunstable: Hillsborough Co., Settled in 1656 as part of Duxbury **MA**, Called Dunstable Township in 1661, **Inc. in 1673 as Dunstable MA, Became Dunstable NH in 1746, Name changed in 1836 to Nashua**

Dunstable Land Grant: Hillsborough Co., **See Hudson & Nashua**

Dunstable Township: Hillsborough Co., **See Dunstable & Nashua**

Durham: Strafford Co., Settlement in 1635 called Oyster River P. 1 of 3 V. in Dover, **Inc. in 1732 as Durham**

East Andover: Merrimack Co., Settled in 1761, **A V. in Andover**

East Town: Carroll Co., Settled in 1749, **See Wakefield**

Emerisstown: Merrimack Co., Settled in 1761, **See Andover**

Epping: Rockingham Co., Settled in 1710 as part of Exeter, **Inc. in 1741 as Epping**

Exeter: Rockingham Co., Settled in 1638 by Rev. John Wheelwright and his followers, **Inc. in 1638 as Exeter**

Farmington: Strafford Co., Settlement in 1728 as part of Northwest Parish in Rochester, **Inc. in 1798 as Farmington**

Fisherville: Merrimack Co., Settled in 1725, **See Penacook and Concord (2)**

Fitzwilliam: Cheshire Co., Settled in 1710 as part of Exeter, **Inc. in 1741 as Fitzwilliam**

Foss Beach: Rockingham Co., Settled in 1630, **Alias for Rye**

Gilsum: Cheshire Co., **Inc. in 1763 as Gilsum**, Settled in 1764

Goffstown: Hillsborough Co., Settlement in 1734 called Narragansett No. 4 (**MA & NH** disputed territory), **Inc. in 1761 as Goffstown NH**

Gosport: Rockingham Co., Settlement in 1623 as a V. on Star Island in the Isles of Shoals, **Inc. in 1715 as Gosport,** Note: (Gosport is the only community in the Isles of Shoals to ever be incorporated as a town.)

Great Island: Rockingham Co., Settled in 1623 as a part of Portsmouth, A V. in Portsmouth in 1679, **Inc. in 1693 as New Castle**

Greenland: Rockingham Co., Settled in 1638 as part of Strawberry Banke, A V. in Portsmouth in 1653, **Inc. in 1721 as Greenland**

Gunthwaite: Grafton Co., Settled in 1763, **See Lisbon**

Hampton: Rockingham Co. Settlement in 1638 called Winnacunnet P. (Massachusetts Bay Colony), **Inc. in 1639 as Hampton MA,** In Norfolk Co. MA in 1643, **Ceded to NH and in Rockingham Co., in 1679**

Hampton Falls: Rockingham Co., Settled in 1638 as part of Hampton **MA**, Ceded to **NH** in 1679, **Inc. in 1726 as Hampton Falls**

Hampstead: Rockingham Co., Settlement in 1640 called Timberline Parish in Haverhill and Amesbury **MA**, Ceded to **NH** in 1679, **Inc. in 1749 as Hampstead NH**

Hancock: Hillsborough Co., Settled in 1764 as part of Peterborough, **Inc. in 1779 as Hancock**

Hill: Merrimack Co., Settlement in 1753 called New Chester in Grafton Co., **Inc. in 1753 as New Chester in Grafton Co., Name changed to Merrimack (1) in 1837, Name changed to Hill in 1941**, Hill relocated in 1941 to Merrimack Co. due to the Franklin Falls dam project

Hillsborough: Hillsborough Co., Settlement called Number Seven in 1735, **Inc. in 1772 as Hillsborough**

Hilton's Point: Strafford Co., Settlement in 1624 by Edward and William Hilton called Hilton's Point, **See Dover**

Hinsdale: Cheshire Co., Settlement in 1742 called Fort Hinsdale, **Inc. in 1753 as Hinsdale**

Holles: Hillsborough Co., Settlement in 1731 called Holles, **Inc. in 1746 as Holles,** About 1775, the spelling of Hollis began to be used and after 1815 only the spelling Hollis is seen officially.

Hollis: Hillsborough Co., **Alias of Holles**

Hopkinton: Merrimack Co., Settlement in 1736 called New Hopkinton due to another Hopkinton in **MA, Inc. in 1765 as Hopkinton NH**

Hudson: Hillsborough Co., Settled in 1656 as part of the Dunstable Land Grant, **Inc. in 1673 as Hudson**

Isles of Shoals: Rockingham Co., Settlement of nine habitable islands began prior to 1623 called Isles of Shoals, All nine were Inc. in 1661 as Appledore by Massachusetts Bay Colony, Later, four Islands (Star, Lunging, Seavey & White) were deemed to be in **NH** (Portsmouth) while five (Appledore, Cedar, Duck, Malaga & Smuttynose) were in **ME** (Kittery), **See Appledore & Gosport**

Jaffrey: Cheshire Co., Settlement in 1736 as part of Rowley-Canada, Called Jaffrey V. in Monadnock No. 2 in 1749, **Inc. in 1773 as Jaffrey**

Keene: Cheshire Co., Settlement in 1736 called Upper Ashuelot **MA**, Called Upper Ashuelot, **NH** in 1741, **Inc. in 1753 as Keene**

Kingstown: Rockingham Co., Settled in 1674 as part of Hampton, **Inc. in 1694 as Kingstown**

Lampreyville: Rockingham Co., **See Newmarket**

Landaff: Grafton Co., Settled in 1764, **Alias of Llandaff**, The alias Landaff has been officially used for many generations

Lebanon: Grafton Co., Settlement in 1761 called Lebanon, **Inc. in 1761 as Lebanon**, Note: (Many of Lebanon's settlers were from Lebanon CT.)

Lee: Strafford Co., Settled in 1657 as part of Dover, Called Lee V. in Durham in 1712, **Inc. in 1766 as Lee**

Limerick: Cheshire Co., Settled in 1752, **See Stoddard**

Lisbon: Grafton Co., Settlement in 1763 called Concord (1), Called Chiswick in 1764 so Rumford could incorporate as Concord (2) in 1765, Called Gunthwaite in 1768, **Inc. in 1824 as Lisbon**

Littleton: Grafton Co., Settled in 1769 as part of Chiswick, Called Littleton V. in Lisbon in 1670, **Inc. in 1784 as Littleton**

Llandaff: Grafton Co., Settlement in 1764 called Whitcherville, Granted to Dartmouth College in 1770, **Inc. in 1774 as Llandaff,** The alias Landaff has been officially used for many generations

Lyndeborough: Hillsborough Co., Settlement in 1734 called Salem-Canada, **Inc. in 1764 as Lyndeborough**

Madbury: Strafford Co., Settlement in 1699 called Barbadoes V. in Dover, Part of Durham V. in 1716, Called Madbury V. in Durham in 1732, **Inc. in 1775 as Madbury**

Manchester: Hillsborough Co., **Inc. in 1727 as Tyngstown MA later ruled invalid,** Called Tyngstown NH in 1741, **Inc. in 1751 as Derryfield NH, Name changed to Manchester in 1810**

Merrimac: Hillsborough Co., **Alias of Merrymac**

Merrimack (1): Grafton Co., **See Hill**

Merrimack (2): Hillsborough Co., Settlement about 1690 called Merrymac, **Inc. in 1746 as Merrymac** aka Merrimac, Officially spelled as Merrimack since 1914

Merrymac: Hillsborough Co., **See Merrimack (2)**

Milford: Hillsborough Co., Settled in 1733 as a part of Amherst, **Inc. in 1794 as Milford**

Milton: Strafford Co., Settled in 1728 as A V. in the Northwest Parish of Rochester

Monadnock No. 1: Cheshire Co., Settled in 1736, **See Rindge**

Monadnock No. 2: Cheshire Co., Settled in 1736, **See Jaffrey**

Monadnock No. 3: Cheshire Co., Settled in 1760, **See Dublin**

Monadnock No. 6: Cheshire Co., Settled in 1767, **See Nelson**

Monadnock No. 7: Cheshire Co., Settled in 1752, **See Stoddard**

Narragansett No. 3: Hillsborough Co., Settled in 1733, **See Amherst**

Narragansett No. 4: Hillsborough Co., Settled in 1734, **See Goffstown**

Nashua: Hillsborough Co., Settled in 1655 as part of the Dunstable Land Grant in **MA,** Part of Dunstable Township in **MA** in 1661, Northern part of Dunstable Inc. in 1673 in **MA, Inc. in 1746 as Dunstable NH, Name changed to Nashua in 1836**

Nelson: Cheshire Co., Settlement in 1767 called Monadnock No. 6, **Inc. in 1774 as Nelson**

New Bradford: Merrimack Co., Settled in 1771, **See Bradford**

New Breton: Merrimack Co., Settled in 1761, **See Andover**

New Castle: Rockingham Co., Settlement in 1623 called Great Island, Called Great Island V. in Portsmouth in 1679, **Inc. in 1693 as New Castle**

New Chester: Grafton Co., Settlement in 1753 called New Chester, **Inc. in 1753 as New Chester** in Grafton Co., **Name changed to Merrimack (1) in 1837, Name changed to Hill in 1941,** Hill relocated in 1941 to Merrimack Co. due to the Franklin Falls dam project

New Hopkinton: Merrimack Co., Settled in 1736, **See Hopkinton**

New Ipswich: Hillsborough Co., Settlement called New Ipswich in 1738 settled by 60 families from Ipswich, MA, **Inc. in 1762 as New Ipswich**

Newfields: Rockingham Co., Part of Exeter in 1635, Settlement in 1638 called Newfields in Exeter, Called Newfield V. in 1681, Called South Newmarket a V. in Newmarket in 1727, **Inc. in 1849 as Newfields**

Newington: Strafford Co., Settlement in 1640 called Bloody Point in Dover, **Inc. in 1764 as Newington**

Newmarket: Rockingham Co., Prev. to 1727 called Newmarket in Exeter, **Inc. in 1727 as Newmarket aka Lampreyville**

North Monadnock: Cheshire Co., Settled in 1760, **See Dublin**

Northam: Stafford Co., **See Dover**

Northwest Parish: Strafford Co., Settled in 1728, **See Farmington and Milton**

Northwood: Rockingham Co., Prev. to 1763 part of Nottingham, Settlement in 1763 called Northwood, **Inc.in 1773 as Northwood**

Nottingham: Rockingham Co., **Inc. in 1722 as Nottingham**

Number Seven: Hillsborough Co., Settled in 1735, **See Hillsborough**

Odiorne Point: Rockingham Co., A fishing V. in 1623, A V. in Rye in 1727

Oyster River: Strafford Co., A fishing V. in 1623, 1 of 3 Villages in Dover, The site of the worst massacre in NH during the French and Indian War in 1694 with 104 residents killed and 27 taken prisoner.

Oyster River P.: Strafford Co., Settled in 1635, **See Durham**

Pannaway: Rockingham Co., Settled in 1623, **See Rye**

Pelham: Hillsborough Co., Settled in 1722 as part of Dunstable **MA, Inc. in 1746 as Pelham NH**

Penacook: Merrimack Co., Settlement in 1725 called Penacook a V. in Concord aka Fisherville, **See Concord (2)**

Peterborough: Hillsborough Co., Settlement in 1749 called Peterborough, **Inc. in 1760 as Peterborough**

Plaistow: Rockingham Co., Settlement in1728 called Plaistow, **Inc. in 1749 as Plaistow**

Portsmouth: Rockingham Co., Settled in 1623, Called Strawberry Banke in **MA** in 1630, **Inc. in 1653 as Portsmouth**

Protectworth: Sullivan Co., Settled in 1769, **See Springfield**

Rindge: Cheshire Co., Settled in 1736 as part of Rowley-Canada, Called Monadnock No. 1 in 1749 aka South Monadnock, **Inc. in 1768 as Rindge**

Rochester: Strafford Co., Settlement in 1728 called Rochester Village, **Inc. in 1732 as Rochester**

Rochester Village: Strafford Co., **See Rochester**

Rowley-Canada: Cheshire Co., Settlement in 1736 called Rowley-Canada, **See Jaffrey and Rindge**

Rumford: Merrimack Co., Settlement in 1725 called Penacook, **Inc. in 1734 as Rumford, Renamed Concord (2) in 1765**

Rye: Rockingham Co., Settlement in 1623 called Pannaway aka Sandy Beach and Foss Beach, **Inc. in 1727 as Rye**

Salem-Canada: Hillsborough Co., Settlement in 1734 called Salem-Canada, **See Lyndeborough**

Sandy Beach: Rockingham Co., **Alias for Rye**

Seabrook: Rockingham Co., Settled in 1638 as part of Hampton **MA,** Transferred to **NH** in 1679 when Bristol Co. **MA** was abolished, **Inc. in 1768 as Seabrook**

Sligo: Strafford Co., **Alias for Somersworth**

Somersworth: Strafford Co., Settled in 1623 as part of Dover, A V. in Dover in 1700, Called Parish of Somersworth in 1729 aka Sligo, **Inc. in 1754 as Somersworth**

Souhegan No. 3: Hillsborough Co., Settled in 1733, **See Amherst**

South Monadnock: Cheshire Co., Settlement in 1736 called South Monadnock, **See Rindge**

Springfield: Sullivan Co., Settlement in 1769 called Protectworth, **Inc. in 1794 as Springfield**

Squamscott Patent: Rockingham Co., Prev. to 1631 called Winnicutt, Settlement in 1631 called Squamscott Patent, **See Stratham**

Star Island: Rockingham Co., Settled in 1623, Largest of the four Isles of Shoals islands in NH, **See Isles of Shoals & Gosport**

Strafford: Strafford Co., Settled in 1773 as part of Barrington, **Inc. in 1820 as Strafford**

Stratford: Coos Co., Settlement in 1762 called Woodbury, **Inc. in 1762 as Woodbury, Renamed Stratford in 1773**

Stratham: Rockingham Co., Prev. to 1631 called Winnicutt, Called Squamscott Patent in 1631, **Inc.**

in 1716 as Stratham

Strawberry Banke: Rockingham Co., Settled in 1630 as a V. in **MA**, A V. in 1643 in Norfolk Co. **MA MA,** Became a V. in Portsmouth **NH** in 1679 when "Old" Norfolk Co. was abolished, Became a 10-acre history museum in 1951 in Portsmouth

Stoddard: Cheshire Co., Settlement in 1752 called Monadnock No. 7 aka Limerick, **Inc. in 1774 as Stoddard**

Sullivan: Cheshire Co., Settled in 1787, **Inc. in 1787 from parts of Gilsum, Keene, Nelson and Stoddard**

Timberline Parish: Rockingham Co., Settled in 1640, **See Hampstead**

Tyngstown: Hillsborough Co., Settlement in 1727 called Tyngstown, **Inc. as Tyngstown in 1727 in MA later ruled invalid,** See Manchester

Upper Ashuelot: Cheshire Co., Settled in 1736 as a V. in **MA**, Called Upper Ashuelot in 1741 a V. in **NH,** see Keene

Wakefield: Carroll Co., Settlement in 1749 called East Town, **Inc. in 1774 as Wakefield**

Wecohamet: Strafford Co., **See Dover**

Whitcherville: Grafton Co., Settlement in 1764 called Whitcherville, **See Llandaff**

Winnicutt: Rockingham Co., Settlement in 1631 called Winnicutt, **See Stratham**

Woodbury: Coos Co., Settlement in 1762 called Woodbury, **Inc. in 1762 as Woodbury, Renamed Stratford in 1773**

CHAPTER V
RHODE ISLAND

The name Rhode Island originated from the Dutch explorer Adrian Block who named it "Roodt Eylandt" (Red Island) in 1614. The red was due to the red clay that lined the shore.

Colonial Era Events in Rhode Island

1625: **Trading Post Established;** A Dutch trading post on Conanicut Island in present-day Jamestown was established as an extension of the trading activities of the Dutch West India Company.

1635: **First European Settlement;** The Rev. William Blaxton (aka Blackstone) of the Anglican Church immigrated to the New World in 1623. About 1625, he was the first settler on a large tract on what would become Boston Common and Beacon Hill. In 1630, he invited residents of Charlestown to move to his land where they could find the fresh water they wanted. His invited guests soon informed him that his land was owned by the Massachusetts Bay Colony. The Colony then deeded him 50 acres, which he promptly sold back to the Colony. Feeling threatened by his Anglican support of the Church of England, the intolerant puritans burned down his home in 1635. He then moved 35 miles south to a hill overlooking what is now the Blackstone River and became the first settler of what would become Rhode Island. There is a monument marking his grave in Cumberland Rhode Island.

1636: **Providence Founded;** Rev. Roger Williams sought sanctuary after being exiled in 1636 from the Massachusetts Bay Colony for radical religious views and sedition against the Crown. He purchased land from the Narragansett Indians across the Seekonk River and began a new settlement at what would become Providence, Rhode Island

1638: **Pocasset (later Portsmouth) Settlement;** Anne Hutchinson and her disenfranchised followers deemed to be Antinomians (Those who believe that, under the gospel dispensation of grace, the moral law, is of no use or obligation because faith alone is necessary to salvation.) purchased Aquidneck Island (later called Rhode Island) and founded Pocasset (later called Portsmouth).

1643: **Charter for Providence Plantations;** Rev. Roger Williams received a Charter Patent from the British parliament for Providence, Portsmouth and Newport Colonies, confirming all settlers land claims.

1663: **Royal Charter Granted;** King Charles II grants a Charter for Rhode Island and Providence Plantations and Benedict Arnold is elected its first Governor.

1686: **Dominion of New England;** All of the America Colonies from the Delaware River to Penobscot Bay in Maine were declared one entity, Dominion of New England, by King James II. From the outset, there was mass resistance to that concept because the colonists resented being stripped of rights by anyone, let alone a King who had strong ties to the Catholic Church.

1689: **Dominion of New England Collapses;** After King James II was overthrown in December 1688, the Colonies ousted Dominion officials and reverted to their previous structures and authorities.

1746: **Province of Massachusetts Bay (PMB) territory awarded to Rhode Island;** The Court awarded the PMB towns and villages of Barrington, Sowams, Bristol, East Pawtucket and West Pawtucket to RI who formed a new Bristol County with those communities. Also, the PMB towns of Tiverton and Little Compton joined the preexisting Newport County, RI. This action resolved all existing border disputes between PMB and RI.

RHODE ISLAND SETTLEMENTS

<u>Populated Place</u>

Barrington: Bristol Co., Settled in 1667 as part of Swansea **MA**, Inc. in 1717 as Barrington **MA**, Ceded to **RI** in 1747 as part of Warren, **Inc. in 1770 as Barrington**

Block Island: Washington Co., Named Block Island in 1614 Dutch explorer Adrian Block, **See New Shoreham**

Bristol: Bristol Co., Settlement in 1680as a V. in Plymouth Colony **MA**, A V. in 1685 in Bristol Co. **MA**, Ceded to **RI** in 1747

Burrillville: Providence Co., Settled in 1662 as part of Gloucester **RI. Inc. in 1806 as Burrillville**

Charlestown: Washington Co., Settled in 1661 as part of Misquamicut, Called West Charlestown in 1669 a part of Westerly, **Inc. in 1738 as Charlestown**

Conanicut Island: Newport Co., Called Dutch Island in 1636, Settlement soon after 1638 called Conanicut Island, **See Jamestown**

Coventry: Kent Co., Settled in 1642 as part of Shawhomett, Part of Warwick in 1648, **Inc. in 1741 as Coventry**

Cranston: Providence Co., Settled in 1638 as part of the Pawtuxet Purchase, **Inc. in 1754 as Cranston, Inc. in 1910 as city of Cranston**

Cumberland: Providence Co., Settled in 1635 as part of Rehoboth **MA, Inc. in 1747 as Cumberland RI**

Dutch Island: Newport Co., Settled in 1638 aka Conanicut Island, **See Jamestown**

East Greenwich: Kent Co., Settled in 1640 as part of Elizabeth's Neck in **CT,** Part of Greenwich **CT** in 1665, 5,000 acres of Greenwich **CT** awarded to **RI** in 1677 and **Inc. as East Greenwich RI**

East Providence: Providence Co., Settled in 1636 as the western part of Rehoboth **MA**, The western part of Seekonk **MA** in 1812, Western part of Seekonk **MA** ceded in 1862 to **RI, Inc. in 1862 as East Providence RI**

East Town: Carroll Co., Settled in 1749, **See Wakefield**

Exeter: Washington Co., Prev. to 1674 part of Little Rest, A V. in 1722 in the wesrtern part of North

Kingston, **Inc. in 1743 as Exeter**

Foster: Providence Co., Prev. to 1662 called West Quanaug, Settlement in 1662 called Foster, A V. in the western part of Scituate in 1730, **Inc. in 1781 as Foster**

Gloucester: Providence Co., Settled in 1636 as part of Providence, **Inc. in 1731 as Gloucester**

Hopkinton: Washington Co., Prev. to 1661 part of Misquamicut and also part of the area that would become Westerly that was in dispute by **RI, CT,** and **MA,** King Charles dissolved all claims in 1665 and renamed the area King's County in **RI,** The General Assembly of **RI** then **Inc. King's County in 1669 as Westerly** and Westerly immediately organized itself into four areas: Westerly, West Charlestown, Richmond and Hopkinton, The Richmond area was **Inc. in 1747 as Richmond, Named Hopkinton in 1757**

Jamestown: Newport Co., A Dutch fur trading post in 1636 called Dutch Island, Called Conanicut Island in 1638 and used as grazing land for sheep, Settlement soon after 1638 called Conanicut Island, **Inc. in 1678 as Jamestown**

Johnston: Providence Co., Prev. to 1759 part of Providence, **Inc. in 1759 as Johnston**

King's County: Washington Co., Settled in 1665, **See Westerly, West Charlestown, Richmond and Hopkinton**

Kingstown: Washington Co., Settlement in 1674 called Kingstown, **Inc. in 1674 as Kingstown, Name changed to Rochester in 1686, Name changed back to Kingstown in 1689, Kingstown split in 1722 and reincorporated as North Kingstown and South Kingstown**

Kingston: Washington Co., **See Little Rest**

Little Compton: Newport Co., Settlement in 1675 called Sakonnet, **Inc. in 1682 as Little Compton** by Plymouth Colony, Ceded to **RI** in 1747 becoming part of Newport Co.

Little Rest: Washington Co., Prev. to 1674 part of a V. called Little Rest, Name changed in 1826 to Kingston a V. in South Kingstown

Manisses: Washington Co., **See New Shoreham**

Middletown: Newport Co., Settled in 1638 as part of Newport, A V. in Newport in 1731, **Inc. in 1743 as Middletown**

Misquamicut: Washington Co., Settled in 1661, **See Westerly, Charlestown, Richmond and Hopkinton**

New Shoreham: Washington Co., Named Block Island in 1614 Dutch explorer Adrian Block, Part of Massachusetts Bay Colony (MBC) in 1636, Prev. to 1661 called Manisses by Niantic Indians, Settlement called Block Island in MBC in 1661, **Inc. in 1672 as New Shoreham RI**

Newport: Newport Co., Settlement in 1638 called Newport by the founding families that came from Portsmouth, **Inc. in 1639 as Newport, Inc. in 1784 as City of Newport**

Niswosakit: Providence Co., Part of Woonsocket in 1661, **See Woonsocket**

North Kingstown: Washington Co., Settled in 1674 as part of Kingstown, **Inc. in 1722 as North Kingstown**

North Providence: Providence Co., Settled in 1636 as part of Providence, Part of Providence and Pawtucket in 1671, **Inc. in 1765 as North Providence**

Pawtucket: Providence Co., Settled in 1671 as a V. called Pawtucket in Rehoboth, **MA,** Merged in 1860 with West Pawtucket **MA** and ceded to **RI, Inc. in 1862 as Pawtucket RI, Inc. in 1954 as City of Pawtucket**

Pocasset: Newport Co., **See Portsmouth**

Portsmouth: Newport Co., Sett;ement in 1638 called Pocasset by religious dissenters from Massachusetts Bay Colony, **Inc. in 1639 as Portsmouth**, See above 1638 "Colonial Events in Rhode Island"

Providence: Providence Co., Settlement in 1636 called Providence the first European settlement in **RI** founded by religious dissenters from Massachusetts Bay Colony led by Rev. Roger Williams, 1636 Inc. in 1636 as Providence, Inc. in 1832 as City of Providence

Richmond: Washington Co., Prev. to 1661 part of Misquamicut, Settlement in 1661 as part of the area that would become Westerly that was in dispute by **RI, CT,** and **MA,** King Charles dissolved all claims in 1665 and renamed the area King's County in **RI,** The General Assembly of **RI** then **Inc. King's County in 1669 as Westerly** and Westerly immediately organized itself into four areas: Westerly, West Charlestown, Richmond and Hopkinton, The Richmond area was **Inc. in 1747 as Richmond, Named Hopkinton in 1757**

Rochester	Washington			See Kingstown
Sakonnet	Newport	1682		See Little Compton
Scituate	Providence	1710	1731	1710 part of Providence called Satuit by families of settlers from Sciuate MA,
		1731 Inc. as Scituate		
Shawhomett	Kent	1642		See Warwick, Coventry and West Warwick
Smithfield	Providence	1636	1730	1636 part of Providence, 1731 Inc. as Smithfield
South Kingston	Washington		1674	1674 part of Kingstown, 1722 Inc. as South Kingstown
Tiverton	Newport	1629	1694	1629 called Tiverton **MA,** 1694 Inc. as Tiverton **MA,** 1747 ceded to **RI**
Wakefield	Carroll	1749	1774	1749 called East Town
Warren	Bristol	1653	1668	1653 called Sowams **MA,** 1668 Inc. as Sowams **MA,** 1747 with Barrington ceded to **RI** as Barrington, 1770 separated from Barrington and Inc. as Warren
Warwick	Kent	1642	1648	1642 part of Shawhomett, 1643 claimed by **MBC,** 1648 Shawhomett Inc. as Warwick **RI,** 1931 Inc. as <u>city</u> of Warwick

West Charlestown: Washington Co., **See Charlestown**

West Pawtucket		1671	See Pawtucket
West Quanaug	Providence	1662	See Foster
West Warwick	Kent	1642	1642 part of Shawhomett, 1648 part of Warwick, 1913 Inc. as West Warwick

Westerly: Washington Co., Prev. to 1661 part of Misquamicut, Settlement in 1661 as part of the area that would become Westerly that was in dispute by **RI, CT,** and **MA,** King Charles dissolved all claims in 1665 and renamed the area King's County in **RI,** The General Assembly of **RI** then **Inc. King's County in 1669 as Westerly** and Westerly immediately organized itself into four areas: Westerly, West Charlestown, Richmond and Hopkinton,

Woonsocket	Providence	1820	1867	1661 part of Providence called Niswosakit, 1820 called Woonsocket Falls V., 1867 Inc. as Woonsocket, 1888 Inc. as city of Woonsocket
Woonsocket Falls	Providence	1820		1820 a V. in Providence, See Woonsocket

----

CHAPTER VI
VERMONT

The name Vermont comes from the French "Vert Mont" (Green Mountain).

French Exploration	1535	Jacques Cartier is the 1st European to explore what would become Vermont
Territory Claimed by France	1609	Samuel de Champlain claims what would become Vermont as a territory of France
First European Settlement	1666	Fort Ste Anne built by the French at Isle La Motte
First Permanent European Settlement	1724	Fort Dummer built at what is now Brattleboro by PMB Militia
French Build Another Fort	1731	Fort de Pieux built at Chimney Point

1749: **New Hampshire Grants;** Between 1749 and 1764 Gov. Benning Wentworth of the New Hampshire Colony sold 135 land grants between the Connecticut River and Lake Champlain north of Massachusetts. This territory was rightfully claimed by New York, and while New York had done little to settle this territory, they disputed Wentworth's actions and told the newly granted towns that they would have to buy the same land again from New York.

France Cedes Claims to Vermont	1763	Following many years of armed conflict, France cedes all claims to the area to the British
Vermont Becomes part of New York	1764	King George III decreed in July 1764 that the territory in question was part of **NY**, however, Gov. Wentworth of NH made two more grants in Oct. after that ruling (Walker and Waltham)
Fort Ticonderoga Captured	1775	The Green Mountain Boys, led by Ethan Allen and Col. Benedict Arnold, capture Fort Ticonderoga **NY** from the British.

"New Connecticut"	1777	On January 15th, "New Connecticut" is declared an Independent Republic of the Union at the Westminster **NY** (soon to be **VT**) courthouse.
"Independent Republic of Vermont"	1777	WHOOPS! The name New Connecticut is already taken by a town in PA so on June 4th the name of the Independent Republic was changed to Vermont. This "Republic" concept would occur again in Texas and, in similar fashion in California and Hawaii.
Vermont joins the USA	1791	14th State and 1st since the initial 13.

VERMONT SETTLEMENTS

The territory that would become the State of Vermont in 1791 had a difficult and complicated settlement period from 1724 to 1791. Not only did the British and French both claim it until 1763, MA and NY both considered it part of their Colony Patents until the court decided in favor of NY in 1764. After 1764, NY ordered previously settled towns to buy their land again from NY. That unreasonable edict led to the territory becoming The Independent Republic of Vermont in 1777, thanks to Ethan Allen and the Green Mountain Boys.

While a Dutch/British trading post had been established in 1690 near present-day Addison, the first permanent settlement began as a tactical military maneuver with MBC building Fort Dummer on the Connecticut River near present-day Brattleboro in 1724. The next major event came in 1764 when, by Royal Decree, NY prevailed with their claim and MA lost any claim to the land north of Pawtucket Falls (near present-day Lowell) and that decree also set the border with NH as the west bank of the Connecticut River. NY had done little to settle this area then defined as "between Lake Champlain, the Connecticut River and north of Pawtucket Falls". That had left a vacuum that was filled by Gov. Benning Wentworth of NH who had sold 135 New Hampshire Grants (NHG) from 1749 to 1764. From 1764 until 1777 NY initiated very few settlements with only two were found in my research for the following list (Bethel and Royalton). Any settlements from 1777 to 1791 were made as part of the independent republic and had to be reincorporated after Vermont became a State in 1791.

Populated Place		Settled	Grant	
Addison	Addison		1761	1761 **NHG** named Addison
Arlington	Bennington	1764	1761	1761 **NHG** named Arlington, 1777 Capital of "Independent Republic of Vermont"
Bennington	Bennington	1761	1749	1749 **NHG** named Bennington (1st NHG)
Berlin	Washington	1785	1763	1763 **NHG** named Berlin
Bernard	Windsor		1761	1761 **NHG** named Bernard
Bethel	Windsor		1771	1771 Inc. as Bethel **NY**, 1779 Inc. as Bethel **VT**

Brandon	Rutland		1761	1761 **NHG** named Neshobe, 1784 renamed Brandon
Brattleboro	Windham			Alias of Brattleborough
Brattleborough	Windham	1724	1753	1724 site of Ft Dummer, Prev. to 1753 called Wantastiquet, 1753 NHG named Brattleborough, aka Brattleboro
Bridgewater	Windsor	1779	1761	1761 **NHG** named Bridgewater, 1785 Inc. as Bridgewater VT
Bridport	Addison	1768	1761	1761 **NHG** named Bridport
Castleton	Rutland	1770	1761	1761 **NHG** named Castleton
Chittenden	Rutland	1780	1780	1780 Inc. as Chittenden **VT**
Clarendon	Rutland	1762	1761	1761 **NHG** named Clarenden
Dorset	Bennington	1768	1761	1761 **NHG** named Dorset, 1775/1776 Meeting place for the Green Mountain Boys at Cephas Kent's tavern
Dover	Windham	1779	1780	1780 South part of Wardsborough, 1810 Inc. as Dover **VT**
Dummerston	Windham	1724	1753	Prev. to 1753 called Dummerston, **NHG** 1753 named Fulham, Name later changed back to Dummerston
Dupplin	Sullivan		1753	1735 named Number 9 by **MBC**, 1753 **NHG** renamed Dupplin, 1767 renamed Lemster **NY**, 1772 Inc. as Lemster **NY**,
Fairlee	Orange	1766	1761	1761 **NHG** named Fairlee
Fane	Windham		1753	1753 **NHG** named Fane, Grant later voided as it failed to have a town meeting within 5 years of its Charter Grant date
Fayston	Washington	1805	1788	1788 Inc. as Fayston **VT** and sold to a land speculator
Fern Bridge	Addison			See Ferrisburgh
Ferrisburgh	Addison		1762	c 1630 a Dutch Trading Post called Verenbrug (Dutch = ferry bridge) aka Fern Bridge, 1673 abandoned during the 3rd Anglo-Dutch War, 1762 **NHG** named Ferrisburgh
Flamstead	Windsor		1754	1754 **NHG** named Flamstead, Grant later voided because the terms of the Charter were not met, See New Flamstead
Fulham	Windham		1753	1753 **NHG** named Fulham, Name later changed to Dummerston
Glastonbury	Bennington		1761	1761 **NHG** named Glastonbury, 1937 Unincorporated due to lack of residents, 2015 essentially a ghost town with a handful of residents
Guilford	Windham	1760	1754	Prev. to 1754 called Gallups-Canada **MA**, 1754 **NHG** named Guilford, 1758 Inc. as Guilford **NY**, 1791 Inc. as Guilford **VT**
Hamstead	Rockingham	1641	1749	1641 called Timberline Parish in Haverhill **MA**, 1749 **NHG** named Hamstead

Name	County			Notes
Hartford	Windsor		1761	1761 **NHG** named Hartford
Hinsdale	Windham	1753	1764	1753 part of Northfield V. in Hinsdale **NH** that encompassed both sides of the CT River, 1764 (CT River becomes NH/VT boundary) and West side of river is Inc. as Hinsdale **VT** and East side Inc. as Hinsdale **NH**, 1802 Hinsdale VT renamed Vernon.
Jamaica	Windham	1780	1780	1780 Inc. as Jamaica **VT**
Kent	Windham		1770	1770 Inc. as Kent **NY** voided as not settled within the time frame required, See Londonderry
Killington	Rutland		1761	1761 **NHG** named Killington, 1800 renamed Sherburne, 1999 name changed back to Killington
Leicester	Addison	1773	1761	1761 **NHG** 1761 named Leicester
Lemster	Sullivan		1753	1735 named Number 9 by **PMB, NHG** 1753 renamed Dupplin, 1767 renamed Lemster, 1772 Inc. as Lemster
Londonderry	Windham	1780	1780	1770 Inc. as Kent **NY** voided as not settled within the time required, 1780 Inc. as Londonderry **VT**
Manchester	Bennington	1764	1761	1761 **NHG** named Manchester
Marlboro	Windham	1763	1751	1751 **NHG** New Marlborough, 1800 name changed to Marlboro
Middlesex	Washington		1763	1763 **NHG** named Middlesex
Middlebury	Addison		1761	1761 **NHG** named Middlebury
Montpelier	Washington	1787	1818	1818 Inc. as Montpelier, **VT**, 1805 became the State Capital of Vermont, 1818 Inc. as Montpelier, 1895 Inc. as the <u>city</u> of Montpelier
Neshobe	Rutland		1761	1761 **NHG** named Neshobe, See Brandon
New Flamstead	Windsor	1764	1761	1754 **NHG** named Flamstead void because the terms of the Charter were not met, 1761 **NHG** named New Flamstead, 1766 name changed to Chester **NY,** The new VT Legislature kept the name Chester
New Marlborough	Windham	1763	1751	See Marlboro
Newfane	Windham	1766	1761	1753 **NHG** named Fane void as it failed to have a town meeting within 5 years of Charter, 1761 **NHG** named Newfane, 1766 settled by families from Worcester Co., MA
Northfield V.	Windham			See Hinsdale and Vernon
Norwich	Windsor	1765	1761	1761 **NHG** named Norwich
Number 9	Sullivan		1735	1735 named Number 9, 1753 **NHG** renamed Dupplin, 1767 renamed Lemster, 1772 Inc. as Lemster
Pawlet	Rutland		1761	1761 **NHG** named Pawlet

Pittsfield	Rutland	1786	1781	1781 Inc. as Pittsfield VT
Pittsford	Rutland	1769	1761	1761 **NHG** named Pittsford, 1769 settled with 2 Revolutionary War forts built nearby (Ft Mott 1777 and Ft Vengeance 1780)
Pomfret	Windsor	1770	1761	1761 **NHG** named Pomfret
Poultney	Rutland	1771	1761	1761 **NHG** named Poultney
Pownal	Bennington	1730	1760	1760 **NHG** named Pownal
Reading	Windsor	1790	1800	Dates are estimated
Rochester	Windsor	1781	1781	1781 Inc. as Rochester VT
Rockingham	Windham	1753	1752	1752 **NHG** named Rockingham
Royalton	Windsor	1771	1769	1769 Inc. as Royalton **NY**, 1781 Inc. as Royalton in the Independent Republic of Vermont, 1791 became Royalton VT USA
Rutland	Rutland		1761	1761 **NHG** named Rutland, 1886 center of town Inc. as Rutland Village, 1892 Inc. as <u>city</u> of Rutland
Rutland (City)	Rutland		1892	
Rutland Village	Rutland		1761	1886 center of Rutland Inc. as Rutland Village
Salisbury	Addison		1761	1761 **NHG** called Salisbury
Shaftsbury	Bennington		1761	1761 **NHG** named Shaftsbury
Sharon	Windsor	1765	1761	1761 **NHG** named Sharon, 1765 settled with many from Sharon CT
Springfield	Windsor	1763	1761	1761 **NHG** named Springfield
Squawkeag	Windham	1673		See Vernon
Stowe	Lamoille		1763	1763 **NHG** named Stowe, Originally in Chittenden Co., 1810 in Jefferson Co., 1814 Jefferson Co. renamed Washington Co., 1835 in Lamoille Co.
Strafford	Orange		1761	1761 **NHG** named Strafford
Tetford	Orange	1764	1761	1761 **NHG** named Tetford
Timberline Parish	Rockingham	1641		See Hamstead
Tinmouth	Rutland		1761	1761 **NHG** named Tinmouth
Townshend	Windham		1753	1753 **NHG** named Townshend
Tunbridge	Orange	1776	1761	1761 **NHG** named Tunbridge
Verenbrug	Addison			See Ferrisburgh
Vernon	Windham	1673	1723	1673 called Squawkeag, 1714 called Northfield **MA**, 1723 Inc. as Northfield Franklin Co. **MA**, 1753 part of Northfield V. in Hinsdale **NH** Inc.on both sides of the CT River, 1764 (CT River becomes NH/VT boundary) and West side of river is Inc. as Hinsdale **VT** and East side Inc. as Hinsdale **NH**, 1802 Hinsdale VT name changed to Vernon.
Waitsfield	Washington		1782	1782 Inc. as Waitsfield VT
Walker			1764	Along with Waltham the last two grants

				made by Gov. Wentworth of NH in Oct.
Waltham	Addison		1764	See Walker
Wantastiquet	Windham			See Brattleborough
Wardsborough	Windham	1779	1780	1780 Inc. as Wardsborough VT
Waterbury	Washington	1763	1763	1763 **NHG** named Waterbury, 1882 Inc. as Waterbury VT
Westminster	Windham		1735	1735 Inc. as Westminster, Cumberland Co., **NY,** 1791 officially became Westminster Windham Co. **VT** when VT joined the Union
Wilmington	Windham		1751	1751 **NHG** called Wilmington
Windham	Windham		1796	1780 part of Londonderry, 1796 Inc. as Windham
Windsor	Windsor	1764	1761	1761 **NHG** named Windsor, 1777 site of the signing of the Independent Republic of Vermont constitution, State Capital until 1805 when Montpelier became the Capital of Vermont
Woodstock	Windsor	1768	1761	1761 **NHG** named Woodstock, 1837 Inc. as Woodstock **VT**

Glossary of Abbreviations

aka	also known as
Co.	County
Dist.	District
EPR	East of the Penobscot River
est.	established
EUR	East of the Union River
I.	Island
Inc.	Incorporated
MBC	Massachusetts Bay Colony
NHG	New Hampshire Grant
org.	organized
P.	Plantation
PMB	Province of Massachusetts Bay
prev.	previously
reorg.	reorganized
Twp.	Township
V.	Village

Made in the USA
Lexington, KY
08 July 2016